A
Woman's
Choices

Barbara B. Smith
Shirley W. Thomas
Elaine Shaw Sorensen
Carolyn J. Rasmus
Dwan J. Young
Beppie Harrison
Claudia Fuhriman Eliason
Sally Peterson Brinton
JoAnn Ottley
Ardeth Greene Kapp
Vernice Pere
Marilyn Arnold
Eileen Gibbons Kump
Sharon L. Staples
Eleanor Knowles
Jeri J. Winger
Elaine Cannon

A Woman's Choices

The Relief Society Legacy Lectures

Deseret Book

Salt Lake City, Utah

©1984 Deseret Book Company
All rights reserved
Printed in the United States of America

First printing March 1984

Library of Congress Cataloging in Publication Data
Main entry under title:

A Woman's choices.

  Includes index.
  1. Church of Jesus Christ of Latter-day Saints.
Relief Society—Addresses, essays, lectures. 2. Women,
Mormon—Addresses, essays, lectures. 3. Christian life
—Mormon authors—Addresses, essays, lectures. I. Smith,
Barbara B. II. Church of Jesus Christ of Latter-day
Saints. Relief Society.
BX8643.W4W66   1984   267'.44933   83-25517
ISBN 0-87747-999-2

Contents

Preface

A Woman's Choices is a compilation of talks given in the Relief Society Legacy Lecture series. This series started in March 1982, when the Relief Society of The Church of Jesus Christ of Latter-day Saints observed its 140th anniversary. The theme of the celebration was Legacy: Remembered and Renewed, and during the anniversary week, many women were invited to share their talents and skills in special meetings, demonstrations, and concerts, illustrating the great contributions of the women of the Church.

The lecture series begun that week was continued through the following year. Individuals were invited to speak on subjects of their expertise. The varying subjects of the lectures represent choices made and the diligence and dedication of these women—representative of so many—toward achieving excellence in their lives.

President Spencer W. Kimball reminds us: "May you realize that in you is the control of your life and what you are going to be, what you are going to do. Remember that your choices may control to some extent others whose lives will be a part of your life. Remember also that if you succeed, it isn't because of luck. Success comes from faith and work and prayer and from constant righteous effort." (Talk given at the Women's Conference of the Church, September 16, 1978.)

A Woman's Choices presents seventeen women who have achieved in their individual efforts, who have made choices that have brought distinction to themselves and to others whose lives are part of theirs.

Relief Society: A Story of New Beginnings

Barbara B. Smith

"You will receive instructions through the order of the Priesthood which God has established, through the medium of those appointed to lead, guide and direct the affairs of the Church in this last dispensation; and I now turn the key in your behalf in the name of the Lord, and this Society shall rejoice, and knowledge and intelligence shall flow down from this time henceforth; this is the beginning of better days to the poor and the needy, who shall be made to rejoice and pour forth blessings on your heads." (*History of the Church* 4:607.) The Prophet Joseph Smith's prophetic statement made to eighteen members of the Relief Society in the spring of 1842 was the beginning of an epoch, and its influence a story that needs to be told.

Relief Society is a story of new beginnings. It is a story of springtime with its new life budding and growing. It is a story of hope—hope generated by life. All the world quickens in the glory of springtime, and there is a pulsating contagion of new energy. The old gives way to the new. Life begins anew.

1

Relief Society is a story synonymous with the wheels of progress. The spirit of inspiration that guides our organization allows us to respond to needs and to take advantage of new knowledge. Emma Smith, the first president, enjoined the members to seek out and relieve the distressed, to be ambitious to do good, and to divest themselves of every jealousy and evil feeling toward one another.

When Joseph Smith turned the key in behalf of women in Nauvoo, a door of great significance was opened for womankind. Light and knowledge from heaven began to flow down upon women not only in the Church but everywhere, and the wheels of progress provided women with more and more opportunities to take the responsibility for their own lives and thus work out their own salvation and make contributions to the work of society.

Relief Society is a story of many doors. There were doors that closed in England and doors that opened for a brief period in Nauvoo, and now there are doors opening all around the world. And behind each door is a woman whose life is individual, unique, and important.

Relief Society is a story of many dimensions. It is a story of dramatic events. It is a story of humble people in humble homes. It is a story of individual triumph and tragedy, of plodding drudgery, and of magnificent dreams. It is a story of faith. It is a story of women. It is a story of partnership and solitude, of nurturing and caring and sustaining one another. It is a story of personal, spiritual stretching and growing. It is a story of charity. Most of all, Relief Society is a story of love. It is a story of love of women for one another. It is a story of a sweet sisterhood that will last beyond mortal life, that will last forever. It is a story of the love of women for the men in their lives who are a part of the happiness and eternal joy that will continue on and on.

Relief Society is a story of love of a woman for a child. It is told over and over again with each new life, with each accomplishment of a child, and with each heartache. Relief Society is the love of a neighbor in her time of happiness or sorrow. It is a burden shared and lifted. It is the love of knowledge and a better way of life that enriches. Relief Society's love extends as far as arms can reach and as far as thoughts can expand. It ever directs women to Him whose work and glory it is to bring to pass immortality and eternal life to her and those she loves. As President Belle S. Spafford declared, "Relief Society belongs to the past; it belongs to the present; it will belong to the future; it belongs to good women of all nations. Its work is the Lord's work for his daughters."

Relief Society is women—adult women of every culture, tongue, and nation. The backgrounds and experiences of the women are as varied as the flowers of springtime, of summer, and of fall—each a daughter of God with talents and gifts and abilities to add to the other. In the words of Amy Brown Lyman, a former general president of Relief Society, "One of the main objectives of Relief Society from the beginning has been to instill and develop in every member a testimony and spiritual conviction that Jesus Christ is the Son of God; that Joseph Smith was the instrument through which the gospel was restored to earth." As women are nurtured by the word of God, they in turn assume the nurturing role. Each one—each woman, each wife, and each mother—can become an advocate for His children, pleading their cause before Him. It is a divine precedent, as we find ourselves engaged in temporal advocacy on every level.

Jane Wise, a lovely young woman who is an attorney, said to me, "I make my living representing various aspects of the adversarial system, but I never realized the length and breadth of this role in my personal life until the birth of my infant son, who depends on me for almost everything. I am truly his advocate with the world."

In every sister's life is the necessity of confronting alternatives that are basic. To make the best choices, we must become effective advocates. To become the most effective advocates, we must become educated on the choices that confront us each day of our lives in mortality.

To be an effective advocate, we must open doors for those we love. We must understand and learn to work with the most fundamental principles of temporal salvation: self-reliance, personal accountability, and love unfeigned. Relief Society helps define these terms, points out the time and conditions when they will be relevant, and tries to inspire and instruct each sister in such a way that she is provided the impetus to seek for more information and to live according to those commandments she needs most. President Louise Y. Robinson recognized this when she said, "There is always a value in striving, always compensation for effort. When these efforts have an aim to relieve and bless, the result is a gain in priceless experience and a growth in spiritual power."

Relief Society is a constantly renewing story of love. If you would open our record books to any page in any period of time, you would read of the acts of love.

Let's open that door and read from the minutes of a meeting of the Female Relief Society of Nauvoo held July 7, 1843, as a good example:

"Mrs. Pratt mentioned the needy circumstances of Brother Henderson a widower with nine children. . . . She recommended him as an industrious and worthy person. She proposed taking the responsibility of overseeing the cutting and making of clothes, herself being a tailoress."

"Mrs. Durfee presented the case of Porter Rockwell—expressed much feeling of sympathy awakened in her heart by recent recitals of his sufferings—recommended the sisters to unite like the ancient saints in faith and prayer for his deliverance."

"Sister Wooley said she has red yarn which she purposed for a carpet, but thinks it will do more good in mittens, and will contribute it for the sisters to knit."

"Sister Farr has flax which she will contribute."

The Prophet Joseph Smith taught them many things in Nauvoo. In June 1842, he declared, "Nothing is so much calculated to lead people to forsake sin as to take them by the hand, and watch over them with tenderness. When persons manifest the least kindness and love to me, O what power it has over my mind, while the opposite course has a tendency to harrow up all the harsh feelings and depress the human mind." (*History of the Church* 5:24.) President Clarissa S. Williams seemed to reflect these same feelings as she reiterated the counsel of the Prophet to the sisters in her day, saying, "When the Prophet Joseph Smith gave the great mission of love and charity to women, and instructed them to feed the poor and unfortunate, to comfort the sick and the afflicted, he manifested the same spirit as expressed by our Savior and our prophets. Thus he opened the way for women to exercise the motherly instincts inherent in them."

There was a spirit of that instinctive love and tenderness in the Relief Society of Nauvoo, which reached out to warm each heart. Many a person without sustenance was given the generous love of a Relief Society sister. At the fifth meeting of the society a "necessity committee" was formed of members from each ward "to search out the poor and suffering." Members of the committee knocked on every door, often almost filling their fringed carriages as they collected and disbursed supplies. Once a daily milking of a cow was offered and gratefully received.

Rolling west and establishing the Church, making, settling, planting, and creating homes, bringing new life to a desert land—these consumed the Saints' lives for the better part of the rest of the nineteenth century. And Relief Society women continued to teach the message of love in the wilderness.

Eliza R. Snow was instrumental in establishing Relief Society in the new Territory of the Deseret and served as the general president. She urged the sisters to look beyond their circumstances and to bring forth beauty of every kind: "It is not required of women who are seeking to live their religion, gain intelligence and assist in establishing pure and correct principles to neglect their personal appearance. . . . We should seek to increase our fund of knowledge and polish the mind . . . and learn to understand the laws of life."

Under her direction Sarah Kimball, a woman of means who was known for the cultivating of her mind and talents, and who served as Relief Society president in the 15th Ward, opened the doors of her heart and mind, which were full to overflowing with love and kindness. She reported, "This year

I am happy in believing that the needy poor in our city are supplied with a reasonable abundance of fuel, food and raiment." And when she celebrated her seventy-fifth birthday, she sponsored a special dinner for the widows and aged women in her ward, with the women coming in carriages at her expense.

Now let us look into the minute book of the Almo Ward in Cassia Stake in Idaho, March 17, 1892. There we see how the sisters were able to reflect the teachings of President Zina D. H. Young, who urged each sister "to give encouragement to the weak and restrain the erring ones, for the better development and exercise of women's sympathies and charities, that she might have opportunity to attain spiritual strength and power for the accomplishment of greater good in the work of the redemption of the human family." The minutes read: "It is to be hoped that from this time on we will [all] strive to learn from the past wisdom and where we have made mistakes individually or collectively to cover the same with the mantle of charity, peace and good will."

Now we'll turn forward in the minute books to 1921 and read about sisters, having gone through privations themselves, now giving liberally to others. In Liberty Stake in Salt Lake City, they contributed cash to the Jewish Relief Fund and to the County Infirmary. Relief Society sisters in Idaho stakes gathered clothing for the Armenian refugees in Constantinople. Both the general board and some local stakes helped in "making Christmas cheerful" for the Goshute Indians. Relief Society women helped the Red Cross by gathering 15,000 children's garments for the Hoover Fund Campaign in Europe.

Through the years our sisters have sent wheat to China and supplies to help alleviate the suffering caused by the San Francisco earthquake. Minutes of the general board show that in Garfield, Utah, there was such great respect for the competency of Relief Society workers that all relief work there was put under the administration of the society by the Smelter Relief Company, the Utah Copper Cmpany, and the Utah Copper Bank Club, and in Bingham by the Garfield Boarding Houses.

An Arizona Relief Society president, Lenore Smith Rogers, undertook the establishment of a local maternity hospital to give women proper medical care at the time of childbirth.

In Sanpete Stake in Utah, "at the time of a death in the ward, a presidency would make the temple clothes, help prepare the body, and dress it, as well as doing all they could to bring comfort to the bereaved family."

A stake near El Paso, Texas, said, "We do not need a great deal down here, where we are all poor alike."

One ward Relief Society president, a widow with four children, twelve registered Jersey cows, a flock of chickens, a cat, and a horse named Monte, first did her service while driving a surrey or buggy; then she graduated to a used Model T Ford. That Ford was described thus: "Our Model T Ford with the side curtains, poor headlights, no heater, hand-operated windshield wipers. . . . The radiator was frozen up most of the time in cold weather and so were the occupants of the car. When it snowed, we had to hang our heads out of each side of the car to even find the road."

If I were to ask you to tell me of the acts of kindness and love that you or your mothers or grandmothers performed for each other, there would be so many that we would need another granite vault. I know this because human need does not change a great deal, and the love and compassion to meet another's sorrow and pain are not remarkably different. Relief Society sisters are still writing pages in the minute and history books about such fundamental responses as have been noted through these incidents.

The wheels of progress sometimes turn slowly, but ultimately, whether in a surrey or in a Model T or in an LTD, sisters are still anxiously engaged, and their acts of love are found among us still, every day, and for many days when the need is long and lingering.

The necessity committee of those early days in Relief Society expanded to a newer structure in an effort to be better prepared to meet today's challenges, but the fundamentals are still in place. We still walk in partnership in The Church of Jesus Christ of Latter-day Saints. The prophets of the Lord still direct us.

Bathsheba W. Smith had a remarkable confirmation of this direction when, upon the passing of President Lorenzo Snow, she worried that he had not reorganized the Relief Society before he died. Soon after, she had a dream that satisfied her, for she said that the Prophet Joseph Smith was watching over them and she knew that he would look after the Relief Society.

The inspiration of our presidency still forms an ongoing constitution.

Visiting teachers still keep us in touch with each other's needs. Here is a letter that I received from a sister: "Let me tell you about another who truly called upon the powers of heaven while serving as my visiting teacher to greatly strengthen me at the end of my last year of law school. I moved into the Ensign 18th Ward. I attended church and found myself to be the youngest member there by about thirty years. Feeling uncomfortable and not knowing anyone, I drifted into semiactivity. I would appear and disappear in Church like a shadow without exchanging words with anyone.

"In the next few weeks there appeared at my door a vibrant, good-humored, white-haired lady who announced she was my visiting teacher. I received visits from her on an almost weekly basis, many times with other sisters of the ward in tow so that I might become acquainted. Phone calls came when I needed them most; notes and cards magically appeared when I was at my lowest ebb (I was studying to pass the state bar). She was, I later found out to my chagrin, the Relief Society president, but I was no longer a shadow in Church. There was always someone to sit by and someone to talk to. She physically pushed me into a vast army of friends. After having been away from the 18th Ward for several years, I still count its members some of my most cherished friends.

"It was later that I found out the true love and concern that this dear visiting teacher, Sister Kinder, had infused into her stewardship. Many times on her knees, she drew on the powers of heaven to find out from our Heavenly Father how she could best serve me. Her prayers were answered, and resultant blessings to me have not stopped flowing."

In addition to visiting teaching, we have classes that give us other opportunities to teach and at the same time learn of the love that augments the acts of caring and sharing that occur in our classrooms. As President Emmeline B. Wells said, "The development of women in many directions of thought and work and the advancement that has characterized the movement in uplifting the mind and soul is incalculable."

Sister Greenwood was a classic example. She probably did not fully sense her need for spiritual strength when she indicated her willingness and her desire to teach the Spiritual Living lessons. She knew she was not prepared, but she would study hard and fast and pray for the Spirit of the Lord to bless her. She did those things, and in addition, she gave each lesson to her children before she presented it at Relief Society. The members of the class found themselves growing as they watched her grow in knowledge and faith. They wept when she shared with them that it had been determined that she had cancer and that it was incurable. Though she didn't want to leave her husband and her children, she was grateful beyond words of expression for each lesson she had given to her beloved children. She knew her faith and testimony would be able to sustain them through the difficult times that were ahead for them. She also knew that her work as an advocate with the world would end, but she would continue to assume that mighty role for them in the eternities.

This is a new era for women, a time of greater opportunities for women, of more possibilities for expanding the reaches of the mind and the heart. There is a new sound in Relief Society, with sisters today from many nations speaking multiple languages. There is a new urging for each sister to commit herself to a lifetime of learning. Relief Society can serve to motivate and to help in that learning.

During the past eight years I have seen this society become an important factor in the ongoing developments in the

Church organizational patterns. These changes reflect continuing revelation and direction from the Lord, and they must do so in order to meet the awesome challenges of rapid growth and internationalization and at the same time to unify and correlate the Relief Society organization, with its diverse cultures and countries and customs, into the wholeness of the gospel plan.

Originally the Relief Society was organized to provide a way for the women of the Church to do their part and, in a more efficient way, give loving service to meet the needs of the poor and the needy in those difficult days in Nauvoo.

There are stresses in our day, and the same great need for women to do their part. The prophet has introduced Church government by councils, and here women participate, beginning with the council in the home and extending to councils at every level of the Church. They are to help plan and to deliberate together for the shaping of appropriate actions in the various areas and segments of Church population.

Women are still functioning well in this setting. We saw this in one such council when a Relief Society president was assigned to work with a large number of Vietnamese refugee babies who were coming in the night to a camp in southern California. Almost as the landing wheels of the aircraft touched down, Relief Society presidents were alerted, and before dawn a corps of women were there caring for the frightened infants, bathing, feeding, comforting. Hourly the sisters immersed their hands and arms in iodine solution to inhibit the spread of disease from the infections that many of the babies carried. One sister reported how she wept as she tried to bathe two little children who would not let go of each others' hands for fear of losing one another.

Participation of Relief Society members also helps to shape our larger community.

Events of the International Women's Year, the White House Conference on Families, the National Council and International Councils of Women, and the American Mothers, Inc., have involved us in meaningful projects for children and for helping the aged to productively meet their challenges.

As guests on the Phil Donahue television show and through anti-ERA speeches, Relief Society as an organization, and Latter-day Saint women as a group, have become strong advocates for moral family life.

We saw a fulfillment of the prophecy of Joseph Smith made in behalf of Relief Society women, that "queens would be in our midst," when the Queen of Thailand and her entourage came through the doors of the Relief Society Building in Salt Lake City. She was particularly responsive to displays instructing sisters in ways to care for the temporal needs of their families, because she was traveling in behalf of the destitute of her country. She was looking for ways to help them, and our hearts went out to her as she longed to bless her people with bounties appropriate to their wants.

A queen of another sort was Dee Jepsen, liaison on women's issues for President Ronald Reagan. Strengthening community relationships came as a natural result of our invitation to her. Interested in seeing various women's groups in action, she was pleased to attend a meeting of the Relief Society general board and to dine with representatives of many civic groups. During her two-day visit to Salt Lake City, we had the opportunity to show her our impressive building. We also took her through the Church office and administration buildings and let her see Welfare Square. We now have an ongoing dialogue with her and with other leaders who were gathered here on that memorable occasion.

Yes, it is fitting that the Relief Society story should primarily be a story of love, written on many pages by many people, because He said, "By this shall all men know that ye are my disciples, if ye have love one to another." (John 13:35.) His love should recall to our minds the greatest act of love of all time: the atoning sacrifice He performed for us, which opened the door to our resurrection. The joyful message from on high is "He is risen. The tomb is empty. He has conquered death and redeemed all mankind."

I feel sure that it is no accident that Easter, the time when we commemorate His resurrection, is so close to the anniversary of Relief Society. It may well be our reminder that it was to the women that Christ appeared after His crucifixion, and that His heavenly gift to all women should cause us to rededicate ourselves to the principle of love, which directed their lives and His. We probably will never find out all there is to know about love, but much of what we need to learn will come when we follow the grand key words of Relief Society, "Do the work ye have seen me do." Our story will continue with every act of love and every deed of compassion performed by a Relief Society sister. It is a divine love story that will never cease to be.

President Kimball has stated, "To be a righteous woman during the winding-up scenes on this earth, before the second coming of our Savior, is an especially noble calling. The righteous woman's strength and influence today can be tenfold what it might be in more tranquil times. She has been placed here to help to enrich, to protect, and to guard the home." (*My Beloved Sisters,* Deseret Book, 1979, p. 17.) May we accept this magnificent responsibility. In the words of President David O. McKay, "We praise Thy name, O Lord, for the organization of Relief Society of the Church of Jesus Christ of Latter-day Saints, for the thousands [now a million and a half] of loyal, faithful, beautiful women who compose its membership. Their devotion to duty is never-ending; their loyalty to Thee and Thy Priesthood unquestioned; their ministrations to the sick and to the needy untiring; their sympathetic, gentle services give hope to the dying, comfort and faith to the bereaved. O Father, bless these, thy choice handmaidens!"

May we as His daughters go forth armed with His power, with His name upon our lips, with His glory round about us, and with His angels having charge over us.

Barbara B. Smith has been general president of the Relief Society since 1974. Previously she served on the Relief Society general board as well as in the other auxiliary organizations on stake and ward levels. She is a member of numerous boards and organizations, including the Church Educational System board of trustees; Brigham Young University board of trustees; Welfare Services executive committee; Promised Valley Playhouse advisory committee; Lion House board of advisers; Utah Division of Family Services Child Abuse and Neglect advisory council; Utah Society for the Prevention of Blindness; executive committee of the National Council of Women; and the BYU Women's Research Institute. She has also served as an officer of the American Mothers organization and a member of the National Advisory Committee for the White House Conference on Families. She and her husband, Douglas H. Smith, have four daughters and three sons.

Women of Charity: Belle S. Spafford and Barbara B. Smith

Shirley W. Thomas

In the scriptures, we learn that *the glory of God is intelligence,* or light and truth, and that *the nature of God is love.* We see a relationship in truth and charity that, if not fully understood, is nonetheless instructive to us. It tells us something of learning and of love. As His children, we can have a continual increase of knowledge and intelligence, and the result can be a greater capacity for understanding and caring for and providing for the needs of others. The knowledge we acquire will contribute to godliness when it increases our ability to manifest concern for others. The more we know of truth, the more profoundly we can care for the children of our Heavenly Father; and the more we love others, the more clearly we comprehend eternal truth.

Relief Society has as its motto "Charity Never Faileth," which reminds every member that the end of our learning is "charity out of a pure heart"—the love that never ceaseth to be. My lecture concerns two "women of charity," Belle S. Spafford and Barbara B. Smith, who have presided over the Relief

Society and whose lives "speak." They speak a message of charity.

Sister Belle S. Spafford was committed to learning and coming to the truth. Her family and friends knew well that 9:00 P.M. was her bedtime. She didn't want calls after that time because it was then that she studied the scriptures. Her granddaughter once asked her why she had that habit. She answered, "For two reasons: one, because it is a commandment, and two, because when I get to the other side, I want to have something to talk about with some of the prominent men and women in history."

In the last weeks of her life she both learned and taught the gospel in her home on Sunday mornings. Being too weak to attend church meetings, Sister Spafford was able to partake of the sacrament when two young priests brought it to her home each week. After they had administered the ordinance and she had praised them for the fine way in which they did it, she asked them if they would preach to her, saying, "You know, I need to keep learning too."

With a little encouragement from her family, the boys overcame their trepidation and taught her from the scriptures. After their lesson they asked her to teach them. One boy later testified that it was her instruction on the important role of young men in the mission field that convinced him to serve a mission.

On Sister Spafford's eighty-first birthday, her family asked, "Mother, what have you learned during these eighty-one years?"

She replied: "During the four-score and one years of my life, I have learned that earth life is short; that time is extremely valuable and should not be dissipated; that the teachings of the Church are sound and reasonable and true; that obedience brings sure rewards; that disobedience brings naught but sorrow.

"I have learned that adversity is the common lot of everyone. Life's testing lies in whether or not one is able to overcome and rise above it. I have learned that family ties are sacred. No effort is too great to safeguard them. I have learned that true friendships are the favors that bring flavor and sweet refreshment to life. I have learned that freedom is a priceless heritage. Government of the people, by the people, and for the people must not be allowed to perish from the earth. These things I know of a certainty."

Then she later added, "This I also know of a certainty: I have learned that the inborn natures of male and female differ. This is the supreme law of God. The interests of both are best served when respect is shown for this law."

Relief Society has long had courses of study in a varied curriculum to provide sisters with knowledge. But in the years that Sister Barbara Smith has presided over the society, she has had a special concern that the teachings and training opportunities of Relief Society meet the needs of over one and one-half million members. Great effort has been made to address the particular requirements of sisters of widely varying preparation and experience, sisters in seventy-two countries, speaking at least twenty different languages. She has directed the plan for "Phases of Relief Society," which can respond to needs of sisters in the mission field and developing areas as well as the sophistication of large wards and stakes. The Relief Society organizational structure has also been revised under the direction of President Smith, enabling the society to respond with greater emphasis to the individual needs of women.

Sister Smith's term in office has been given to yet another work that has required a kind of selfless giving that has been unique to her time. Before Pilate, Christ proclaimed His mission as that of witness to truth. (John 18:37.) Sister Smith has been required to bear witness of the Church's position on current issues in countless interviews and media presentations. The thousands of letters that poured into the Relief Society offices following her appearance on the *Phil Donahue Show* attest to the role she has filled in representing to the world the intelligent, charitable Latter-day Saint woman.

Many current issues have had to be dealt with in a public way during the years in which Sister Smith has served. She has been both selfless and fearless in meeting the demands that have thrust her in the public eye, gaining great respect for the position she has urged and for the Church itself. During one of these efforts she was described by one observer as being the first reasoned voice in the anti-ERA campaign.

Through her visible presence in the media, many feel a close relationship with Sister Smith. It is a pleasure to travel with her and have members of the Church, men and women alike, first hesitate and then come and speak to her with a halting, "You are Sister Smith, aren't you?" This is possibly a manifestation of the time in which we live, but the remarkable thing to me is how compelling her manner is to them. It is her love that communicates and confirms their belief in her calling and position.

She has communicated concern for others for as long as those who know her can remember and has also taught her children to do this. Years ago when she was a visiting teacher, she and her companion were assigned to call on an elderly sister whose husband, confined to their home, often sat long hours in a chair before a window overlooking the street. The couple were withdrawn and did not at first receive the visiting teachers into their home, but after the many loaves of bread, plates of cookies, and cakes that came frequently from Sister Smith's kitchen, they began to believe that the monthly visits were an expression of true concern. Their hearts warmed toward the two visiting teachers and their meetings became cordial. But the thing Sister Smith's children remember is their mother's counsel to them to wave at the man in the window whenever they passed his home. Before long he was anticipating their goings and comings before and after school. To his day were added moments of joy, and the children learned a lesson of caring for another's need.

There is an especially lovely line from a song about Nauvoo telling of a people who wanted not only to build a city, but to "set it splendidly." I think of that when, on occasion, as a presidency we are considering board meeting. Sometimes there are reasons we might have decided to cancel it but determine instead that it should be held. I can hear Sister Smith say, "Then let's have it and let's make it a really marvelous meeting," and then she begins to plan what will be a memorable and productive schedule of items for the agenda.

Her daughter describes their family gatherings and outings as never ordinary, always special. When they were younger and they all went on a trip together, each of the children was given a notebook prepared with games, puzzles, and things to do and learn. Even now when Sister Smith returns from one of her many trips, if only for a day before going again, she calls together as many of her family as can come and shares with them the things she has learned or seen or brought back.

Sister Spafford was destined to establish Relief Society as a national organization by bringing attention to its work through the National Council of Women. Her indomitable will and perhaps her destiny to serve in this organization were evidenced in the first meeting of the council that she attended. Not knowing anyone in the group, she went alone to the luncheon session and looked for a place to sit at one of the tables. As she asked, at first one table and then another, if the obviously empty places were taken, she was told that they were being held for someone. As she continued around the room receiving the same answer at each table, it became very clear that the places were not reserved or spoken for, but that she was not welcome.

When the president of the council came into the dining hall, Sister Spafford approached her and asked where she wanted her to sit. The president, quickly sensing what was happening, replied that Sister Spafford was to sit with her at the head table.

In the years to follow Sister Spafford was to secure her place at the head table as presiding officer. Her skills and leadership talents were evident to the women on the council; they began to turn to her not only to preside but also to rewrite their constitution and by-laws. It is a measure of her charitable nature that she could endure the rejection of that body of women in her first encounter with them and then continue in that service to finally embrace them and receive their highest recognition. For many years Sister Spafford served the National Council of Women in major positions and exerted important influence in their policies and in efforts to improve the lot of women in America.

More recently Barbara Smith continues to represent Relief Society in the National Council of Women, currently leading the group in selection of the National Women of Conscience. As an officer in the American Mother's organization, she helped arrange for their first meeting in Salt Lake City. She served with distinction on the advisory committee to the White House Conference on Families. She had a great influence in that body in establishing rules and procedures that kept the conference balanced in its representation of many groups and kept an open forum for all voices to be heard. One of the finest tributes paid her at that time was by an editor of *Better Homes and Gardens* magazine, who, after observing the work of the committee, stated that he believed that Sister Smith was one of the truly great women of our country and that her influence and her presence in the deliberations gave the conference a credibility that it would not otherwise have had.

One of the hallmarks of truly charitable people is their ability to expect from others the same level of concern that they give so lavishly—and in so doing to build those for whom they care. How clearly we see this in Sister Spafford's relationship with her husband, Earl. Each day she was in town, they had lunch together. These were inviolate hours in her demanding schedule. She counted so much on his care of her that after his death she was not fully aware of all the responsibilities she had so long counted on his performing in her behalf. Her family tells lovingly of the time, shortly after her husband's passing, when she went for a long drive and ran out of gasoline. Since he had always seen to it that her car was ready whenever she needed it, she was not accustomed to thinking about gas and empty and full tanks. She couldn't imagine what could be wrong with the car and called a wrecker to tow it to the garage for repairs!

In an example related by Sister Smith's daughter, we see another expression of charity in family relationships and the learning or understanding that must come in order that love can be freely expressed.

Her daughter Catherine, as a young mother, was suffering the loneliness of having a husband in a bishopric and gone many nights in church service. One Friday they had planned to go out together. All was in readiness, including baby in bed and the babysitter standing by, when the phone rang. The young wife said, "Don't answer it. I just know it will mean that you have to go somewhere." He said he had to answer it. He did have to go, but he promised that it would be only a few minutes.

As first one hour passed, then another, hopes for the evening fell, and finally Catherine was in tears. It was then that her mother called, just to ask how she was, not suspecting a problem. At the sound of her mother's voice, Catherine's weeping turned to sobs as she poured out her frustrations of loneliness and promises and plans that seemed to come to naught at the call of the bishop. She sobbed that they hadn't even planted their garden; they had gone only as far as tilling the ground and had never had time to plant the seeds. The Prophet had told them to plant a garden but now it was too late.

Sister Smith listened until the problems were all aired, and then she asked if the husband were happy with his work in the bishopric. The daughter answered, "Oh yes, he loves it." And is he tired when he comes home? "Oh no, he is exhilarated." To this, Sister Smith replied, "Then be grateful that he is happy serving the Lord. Don't worry about the garden right now. He is planting a spiritual garden that will help you through the eternities. Be patient and support him in his call." Catherine said that her troubled feelings passed because she knew that her mother loved her, and in that love she could hear the explanation that brought understanding.

Sister Spafford's concern for others was ever evident in her personal associations with people as well as in the establishment of the social service work of Relief Society. It was her courageous pleading the cause of the unwed mother and her baby that resulted in measures to protect the interests of mother, child, and grandparents in the states of Utah, Idaho, and Nevada. Under her direction, Relief Society set up social welfare agencies in these states with professional personnel to handle adoptions and the care of unwed mothers. Letters and wedding invitations that came to her from scores of recipients of these services attested to the loving concern with which she cared for those in troubled circumstances. She also played a major role in the Indian placement program, and she lovingly followed the progress of the Indian students as some entered Brigham Young University, went on missions, and went to the temple.

During Sister Spafford's long years of service to Relief Society, her charitable work was recognized through numerous awards and honorary degrees. She was widely loved and respected and brought this recognition also to Relief Society and to the Church. At the time of her passing, a member of the Council of Twelve stated his belief that history would prove her to be one of the greatest women of this dispensation.

Sister Belle Spafford directed the erection of the Relief Society Building, a long-awaited dream that was fulfilled. In the *Relief Society Magazine* of December 1945, we read her statement to the sisters: "It is our desire to have the building belong to the women of the Church and to have every Relief Society woman feel the pride of ownership in it, . . . a Relief Society building that shall be monumental and beautiful to adequately serve the members of the Society not only for today but in the years to come." The building was to house the charitable work of the social agencies she organized and established, truly a fitting monument to her life of extraordinary service.

Sister Smith too will be long remembered for a monument, a beautiful garden containing twelve life-sized statues and one central figure of heroic proportions, each one depicting a facet of a woman's life and all bearing witness to the recognition afforded women in the Church. It is fitting that the garden is in Nauvoo, Illinois, where the key was turned in behalf of women. In further remembrance of women and their work in the Lord's plan, the home of Sarah M. Kimball, where the women first met to consider a ladies society, was recently restored under the direction of Relief Society.

Barbara Smith has also directed the creation of an exciting learning center in the Relief Society Building, where women from throughout the world can find direction and inspiration for carrying on the work of Relief Society and bringing added beauty, refinement, and efficiency to their individual lives. It serves also as a model of the learning center she hopes that all will create in their own homes.

Sister Smith's door is always open to Relief Society leaders who come for counsel or to those who come from afar anxious to feel that sense of belonging to a worldwide sisterhood. Often women come to see her because of personal problems. How sensitively she handles this delicate role, gently referring the deeply troubled to appropriate priesthood leaders and always building those who lack encouragement or understanding. Whatever the need, she sees to it that no one leaves her presence without an overwhelming sense of being loved and appreciated.

As each of these women has presided over the Relief Society, each has had a keen and perceptive mind and has been able to speak decisively and forcefully for the cause of women. But each has had a work to do that has been unique for her own day. Each has been called of the Lord for her personal attributes of perfection and for a work that only she could do in her appointed time.

Latter-day Saint women have an important work to do in the Lord's plan, and each one can—must—become a woman of charity. But in each age the Lord has chosen one to be leader, model, exemplar to direct the work of Relief Society, the work of learning and love. Belle Spafford and Barbara Smith are women of intelligence and compassion. They have manifested in their own lives the integration of learning and love and have helped to provide for the sisters of the Church a program that embodies a God-becoming way of seeking truth and light, that we may more fully serve others with a Christlike love.

Yes, charity is the bringing together of knowledge and service, learning and love. If the greatest of the commandments has to do with love of God, its full meaning implies far more than sincerity and good will. He came into the world to establish a kingdom to teach people how to worship the Father in spirit and truth. It is not enough that we love; we must also come to a knowledge of the truth and pray with all the energy of our hearts that we may be filled with that love which is called charity, the pure love of Christ, so that when He comes again, we shall be like Him.

We rejoice in the legacy of Relief Society, which is the great gift of God to the women of the Church, and we give honor and adulation to these two great presidents of Relief Society who have so touched and influenced our own lives. We shall ever be grateful to them.

Shirley Wilkes Thomas was serving as second counselor in the Relief Society general presidency when her husband, Robert K. Thomas, received a call to preside over the Australia Melbourne Mission. She served on the Relief Society general board under both Belle S. Spafford and Barbara B. Smith, and was first chairman of the Relief Society's Resource Center Committee. A graduate of Brigham Young University with a bachelor of science in elementary education and English, she also took graduate courses in library science at the University of Oregon. She taught first grade at a private school in New York City, high school English classes in Oregon and Utah, and classes in foods and nutrition at BYU. She and her husband, a former professor of English and academic vice-president at BYU, are the parents of two sons and a daughter.

The Educated
Woman
Within Us

Elaine Shaw Sorensen

Women today stand at an open door of opportunity in education. At no other time in history have we enjoyed such freedom of self-enrichment and fulfillment. Indeed, the "educated woman" has become the expectation of society. Education for many women has become the key to freedom, creativity, independence, and productivity. It has unlocked doors to fulfillment before unrealized. None would discourage a woman's desire for a "proper education"; indeed it is encouraged to such an extent as to have become very near an inalienable right. The "right" of education for modern women is part of our greatest expectations and visions of ourselves.

For this is our time. Today, the world looks to us as women, and particularly to us as Latter-day Saint women, for a source and foundation of wisdom and leadership. The time is now, and the need is great for our fountains to be full. The values and integrity of future generations are dependent upon our personal enlightenment and strength.

But what is "education"? And who is the educated woman?

The meaning of education is often assumed to be somehow related to going to school or learning as an external experience related to acquiring knowledge or skills helpful toward productivity in society. As women, we sometimes assume that education is an isolated activity external to home and family, and that an educated woman is somehow expected to involve herself in career rather than in raising children.

All too often, when a woman makes the conscious effort to become educated, she perceives her alternatives as the following: (1) to seek fulfillment outside her home, (2) to sacrifice her education in order to rear a family, or (3) to try to balance career and family in some "superwoman" fashion. However, education is much broader, comprehensive, and perhaps more personal. It is not an isolated external experience but a process of life, not to be a burden or a thing to be sacrificed in the name of motherhood, but to be within a woman's awareness and efforts throughout her life, that she may take fulfillment from it wherever she may find herself serving society. However and wherever she may choose to become educated, it is the fact that she has chosen the pursuit that is most important.

Let us begin with a definition and discussion of the term *education*. In its most idealistic sense, education is an unveiling of the natural thirst of the mind and soul, and subsequently their replenishment, refreshment, and expansion. It is a process of learning and teaching, with each of these factors being equally significant. It is a perception of life, that enrichment can be drawn from the existing situation. Considered in its broadest sense, it may occur at school, at home, with family, at church, or even in a moment of solitude with an enlightening thought. Education is more than learning. It is a complex interactive teaching-learning process, a dynamic relationship between teacher's and learner's internal and external environments. Whether she be teacher or learner, or both at the same time, at any level and in any setting, a woman may participate in the education process and thus enjoy its results.

Perhaps we are not speaking to the term *education* as defined by Webster. What we are calling education, one may call enrichment, fulfillment, vision, teaching, learning, or a number of other words. Indeed, education as we now see it encompasses all of these.

Obviously, we are speaking idealistically, but let us not be afraid to dream of the ideal. The educated woman is within each one of us, awaiting her discovery.

The purposes and ultimate goals of education include the development of broader and deeper meaning; increased abilities in insightful thinking; increased proficiency at various skills; greater understanding of principles, others, and self; and acquisition of desired attitudes, appreciations, interests, and truths—all in a continual pursuit of excellence. Education is thus a beautiful process of becoming.

Each teacher and each learner are individuals with different capacities resulting in varying degrees of quality in the process of education. A great teacher may have a less than great learner, or an excellent learner may interact with a barely adequate teacher. In any case, the resultant process of education depends upon the contribution rather than upon the innate quality of each. Each may contribute to the quality of the experience of the other, creating a dynamic relationship.

Thus, the real talent or gift is in the capacity and motivation to learn and then share that learning in this dynamic relationship. I experienced such a relationship recently in an attempt to teach my five-year-old to play the piano. At age five, he cannot read and does not seem to have the attributes of a prodigy. I thought it would be much easier for both of us to begin when he had acquired some reading skills, so I promised to start lessons next year. But he was insistent and ready to learn now, so I called upon my best creativity in helping him to begin to read music. He is learning quickly, enjoying it, and contributing effectively to the teaching-learning relationship. Both of us are partaking of the challenging and exciting experience of education in the process. The experience has actually contributed to my own progress toward becoming educated. The statement that a teacher often learns more than her students is commonly heard. Both teacher and learner can be edified and educated in the dynamic process described earlier.

Both teacher and learner (and one may be both at the same time) bring to the process of education a repertoire of experience that they reorganize and upon which they build. Learning is a continual process of growth, resulting from persistent organization and reorganization of experiences." New meaning is then related to past meanings and experiences, each adding upon and expanding the other. This "line upon line" process continues with bits of knowledge continually fusing toward a totality.

These ideas may seem rather academic and idealistic, but they may actually apply to any learning situation a woman may choose. They require some effort, but mostly they require a vision of our potential and the potential of those we may influence.

A woman involved in her own total education may feel the same stirrings of satisfaction when she learns a new quilting stitch or when she teaches her child to pray as when she composes a poem or passes a college final examination. The concept of considering an idea totally new to the mind, of perceiving an old experience in a different way, of gaining a new skill, or of acquiring a new appreciation is exciting. It is not difficult to see why the celebration of education has endured.

Obviously, learning may exist in many settings and at many levels. There are times when information must be inculcated into a learner's mind and skills must be acquired and evaluated. But today, let us envision a "higher" education in which the learner organizes and integrates not only facts but also attitudes and values.

My training is in nursing. Constantly, I see among my colleagues a vision beyond the scientific principles and skills learned. They are the special ones who exhibit more caring attitudes, who see beyond the task of the day, and who seek greater professional values. I could say the same of many wives and mothers who exemplify the idea that the inner motivation to become truly educated—to open the mind and soul to manifest their natural thirst—is more significant than the learning activity itself.

When education is considered in such a broad sense, we see that there may exist an educated woman who has never entered a university. Such a woman may enter this dynamic teacher-learner interrelationship as teacher, sharing proper values with her child, or as learner, reading an uplifting written word. The education process in uplifting reading can be most important. President Joseph F. Smith asserted: "I . . . admonish the Latter-day Saints everywhere to cease loitering away their precious time, to cease from all idleness. . . . Read good books. Learn to sing and to recite, and to converse upon subjects that will be of interest to your associates, and at your social gatherings. . . . Seek out of the best books knowledge and understanding. Read history. Read philosophy, if you wish. Read anything that is good, that will elevate the mind and will add to your stock of knowledge, and those who associate with you may feel an interest in your pursuit of knowledge and of wisdom." (*Gospel Principles*, Deseret Book, 1939, p. 235.)

I ascribe to the same philosophy of learning that W. Somerset Maugham suggests in describing reading:

> When I get close to any person, I always feel like asking in a whisper, confidentially of course, "Can you read?" I don't mean merely taking a page of print and pronouncing the words. Almost anything that walks on two feet and has hands can do that.
>
> What I mean is can you read in a way that makes you think and finally produce something with the look of your own mind upon it. Can you read history, biography, poetry, fiction, science, or religion until you know man's ways and his general direction, so that you can strike the trail of human progress anywhere and follow it? It is a great accomplishment to be able to read—one young person in a hundred, perhaps, takes pains to learn how to read, and he or she will be heard from.
>
> You see people who think they are reading. They sit and look at the print in some bulky, flabby Sunday paper for an hour, for three hours perhaps, or at some cheap magazine, or at some flashy paperback novel. You see people looking at that sort of thing for hours. They merely want something to lean their feeble minds upon to save them from the effort of thinking. This is not reading.
>
> Read books not to gain information. You can get that, cut and dried, in the encyclopedia. Read not to get ideas, but read mainly to gain intellectual and moral stimulus. Read in this mood and the great books will increasingly

enable you to think out your own ideas. One soon tires of a book that does not make him feel now and then like getting up and walking the floor under the impulse of some larger vision of truth.

In a great library, you get into society in the widest sense. . . . From that great crowd you can choose what companions you please, for in these silent gatherings . . . the highest is at the service of the lowest, with a grand humility. . . . In a library you become a true citizen of the world. ("A Confidential Question," reprinted from *Wisdom Magazine,* in *National Education Association Journal,* April 1965, p. 19.)

It would enhance the library of any woman to include the scriptures as part of her quest for education. President Spencer W. Kimball has admonished, "Study the scriptures. Thus you may gain strength through the understanding of eternal things. . . . We want our sisters as well as our men to be scholars of the scriptures." (*My Beloved Sisters,* Deseret Book, 1979, pp. 7-8.)

Thus, a woman may become educated in a number of ways, from candidacy for an advance degree to personal study in her own home. To a woman educated in the sense described, her title of daily work is irrelevant to her "degree" of education. There are no degrees, for true education is a process of life and not a means to an end. We may see a woman with an advanced college degree choosing the setting of her home as her workplace, just as we may see a college graduate in the working world who is less educated than a woman at home who never took a formal college course, but who seeks to constantly feed the hunger and wonder of her mind and who soars in the fields of her own mind and influence.

While serving a mission in Colombia, South America, I met such a sister, educated in the finest sense. I knew her as Hermana Cabrera. Her tiny two-room home had no heat or electricity. She shared her only water source, a pump in the plaza, with five or six other families. She lived alone with her young son and daughter on the barest subsistence. She had trials unnumbered. As a girl she had attended school only long enough to learn to read. But her educated influence of refinement was evident all around her: in the hand-crocheted tablecloth on the rough wooden table, in the pictures of flowers and loved ones on her walls, in her constant searching

questions and study of the gospel, and in the refined, dig-
nified, mature demeanor of her children.

Among the reasons for the many admonitions given to us
as women to further our education, however we choose to do
so, are that the field of our influence is boundless, and that
only from the source of our own enlightenment can we contribute to the pursuit and achievement of excellence in our
existence. We cannot offer from ourselves what is not there,
any more than water can flow from a dry spring. Excellence is
the loftiest goal of education. Obviously, quality of education
is variable, but this highest form that produces that which is
excellent is all too uncommon.

There are a few precious people in the lives of each of us
who refuse to accept less than the best that can be offered by
themselves, their peers, their students, or their children—not
in a demanding, oppressive way, but in a stimulating, exciting
manner that makes each of us want to reach a bit higher in all
our worthy pursuits toward excellence.

None of us travels the road of our existence by chance.
Every decision, every act, every thought moves the direction
of our lives to one path or another. Strangely, it seems that we
achieve that which we desire most, whether or not that idea is
within our awareness. Thus, even our whims and desires deserve our own greatest scrutiny in our pursuits. Often we may
choose the path of least resistance, but occasionally in those
few glorious moments of enlightenment we are offered a
glimpse of our divine nature and a sight of the eternal path toward excellence.

A woman's influence can be limitless. Some women will
choose formal, traditional routes of education and will contribute to discoveries in science, medicine, industry, and business that will change a part of society; others will write books
or create art that will challenge souls for generations. But
some will make just as significant an impact on humanity by
their educated influence on their own sons and daughters at
their own hearths. Mothers who educate themselves in the
best way they know by their wonder, interest, and exhilaration
are mothers such as Jochebed, who nurtured young Moses;

Elisabeth, who taught John; Mary, who must have tutored Christ; and Lucy Mack Smith, who reared our own prophet Joseph Smith.

Our challenge is to realize that our influence on our peers, our families, and our posterity for generations can be limitless. Because of this marvelous potential and boundless influence, we are constantly warned of Satan's plan to destroy. We cannot compromise.

The constant cry of many mothers is "I do not have the time or the energy!" Yes, the challenge is great, but it does not require much time or even a lot of energy. Instead, a woman's education may require a rechanneling of energy, perhaps a new perception, a greater vision of who she is.

Admittedly, the idealistic ideas offered here have not considered in any detail the practical, but the pragmatic will follow the ideal. Once we have caught the vision, we will develop the practical, each in our own individual creative manner.

With the freedom and fulfillment offered by education comes a wider field of decision than we as women have ever known. Opportunities are boundless. What legacy will we leave to the world? What legacy will we leave to our own sons and daughters? I would take the simple counsel offered by Florence Nightingale: "I would earnestly ask my sisters to keep clear of both jargons now current everywhere . . . about the 'rights' of women, which urges women to do all that men do . . . merely because men do it, and without regard to whether this is the best that women can do; and of the jargon which urges women to do nothing that men do, merely because they are women. . . . Surely woman should bring the best she has, *whatever* that is, to the work of God's world, without attending to either of these cries. . . . Oh, leave these jargons, and go your way straight to God's work, in the simplicity and singleness of heart." (*Notes on Nursing,* London, 1859.)

Education, with its fulfillment of knowledge and enrichment and its promise of excellence, is a desirable goal to any woman. Within each woman is the capacity to strive for improvement and the freedom to choose her own path. Our challenge is to choose a path that will offer to each of us the assurance that our chosen course of life is acceptable and according to the will of God. If we are earnest and obedient in our strivings, we are promised the help and comfort of our Heavenly Father. We are His children, and we are rearing His children. His will is our growth, refinement, progress, and influence for good.

Our challenge is to dream and then do, to "learn and then teach." As James Allen tells us, "Cherish your visions; cherish your ideals; cherish the music that stirs in your heart, and beauty that forms in your mind, the loveliness that drapes your purest thoughts, for out of them will grow all delightful conditions, all heavenly environment; of these, if you but remain true to them, your world will at last be built." (James Allen, *As a Man Thinketh*, Bookcraft, p. 52.)

The potential is within each of us to become educated and to share that education with our children and posterity, that the human condition may be improved and enriched. The door is open for each of us to step onto a trail to eternal progress toward excellence. The educated woman is within each of us. We have only to open our minds and drink the fulfillment and exhilaration that come from the expansion of our souls.

Elaine Shaw Sorensen received a bachelor of science in nursing and a master of science in parent-child nursing, and is pursuing a Ph.D. in the College of Health at the University of Utah. She has worked as a nurse at the Primary Children's Medical Center, the Weber County (Utah) Health Department, and St. Benedict's Hospital in Ogden, Utah, and has taught in the University of Utah College of Nursing. Active in the Utah Nurses Association and Sigma Theta Tau, the national honor society for nurses, she has received awards and honors in both nursing and music. She completed a mission to Colombia and is currently serving the Church as a ward organist and Relief Society social relations teacher. She and her husband, Dr. Clifford G. Sorensen, have four children; the family resides in Layton, Utah.

The Gift and Power of the Holy Ghost

Carolyn J. Rasmus

In September 1978, President Spencer W. Kimball spoke to the women of the Church and said, "To be a righteous woman is a glorious thing in any age. To be a righteous woman during the winding-up scenes on this earth, before the second coming of our Savior, is an especially noble calling. The righteous woman's strength and influence today can be tenfold what it might have been in more tranquil times." (*My Beloved Sisters,* Deseret Book, 1979, p. 17.)

The following year he again spoke to the sisters and said, "Much of the major growth that is coming to the Church in the last days will come because many of the good women of the world (in whom there is often such an inner sense of spirituality) will be drawn to the Church in large numbers. This will happen to the degree that the women of the Church reflect righteousness and articulateness in their lives and to the degree that they are seen as distinct and different—in happy ways—from the women of the world. . . . Thus it will be," he continued, "that the female exemplars of the Church will be a significant force in both the numerical and the spiritual growth of the Church in the last days." (Ibid., pp. 44-45.)

These quotations put in perspective the importance of getting the Spirit and keeping it. As we seek to be righteous and prepare to participate in the winding-up scenes prior to the second coming of the Savior, we need to seek to have the guidance of the Spirit in our lives.

May I share some personal experiences and ideas that I have thought about concerning the gift and power of the Holy Ghost. I am sensitive to the fact that in sharing personal experiences, mine aren't necessarily unique, but because they are mine, I will use them to be illustrative.

I first came to Brigham Young University in 1969, knowing very little about BYU and even less about The Church of Jesus Christ of Latter-day Saints. I was on a one-year's leave of absence from Iowa State University and came to pursue a degree in physical education. I had previously become acquainted with Dr. Leona Holbrook, chairman of the Women's Physical Education Department at BYU. I had heard her speak, and I determined that wherever she was, I would go, because I felt she had things to teach that I couldn't learn from anyone else. One of the problems was that Leona Holbrook knew me, too. She knew that I smoked and drank, but instead of saying to me, "Carolyn, you'd better not come to BYU because you won't fit in," or "We have a Word of Wisdom, and you'll have a problem when you get here," she simply said to me, "Brigham Young University is a unique place, and before you make a decision that this is where you want to go to school, you'd better come and look around." I had an opportunity when I was on my way to Oregon to stop at BYU and spend two days. I noted on a daily calendar, "My stop at BYU only served to convince me that I made the right decision. Having been there made me realize I'll even be able to give up my much-loved wine for what I'll be able to receive in return."

My experiences at BYU were positive and good. I never missed a devotional assembly. I was taken to the Visitors Center in Salt Lake City so many times that I knew the entire dialogue. The thing I did not know was the truthfulness of the messages. After I had been in Utah for almost a year and a half, a friend took me hiking one Saturday in October. Suddenly, in the middle of nowhere, she said, "It is now time for general conference, and I've brought a portable radio." I didn't know how to get back home, so I sat and listened. We didn't talk about it, but that night I wrote this: "Everything sounds so right."

The next day, Sunday, I visited with a friend and told her many thoughts I had had about the Church. We talked about fasting and prayer and together made a decision that we would fast on Monday. I was also planning to study for a statistics test. I hadn't been in a math class for over twenty-five years, so doing well on the first statistics test of the semester was important to me.

As I sat down to study on Monday morning, I could not concentrate on anything. I knew I had to do well on the test, and finally I knelt down to pray. I don't know what I asked in that prayer, but when I sat down to work on my statistics problems, I felt impressed to write something else. On a scrap of paper, I wrote: "October 12, 1970, 8:45 A.M.—Go now, my child, for there is much work to be done. I send my Spirit to be with you to enable you to work and think clearly, to accomplish all that lies before you this day. Go and know that I am with you in all things, and later return unto me, coming to me with real intent of prayer. Know that I am the Lord, that all things are possible to them who call upon my name. Take comfort in these words. Fill your heart with joy and gladness, not sorrow and despair. Lo, I am with you always, even unto the end of the world. Know me as Comforter and Savior."

About noon I took a break. For some reason I felt impressed to read sections 88 through 90 in the Doctrine and Covenants. Now, one cannot be in Utah for a year and a half and not know about the Word of Wisdom, but I did not know it was found in section 89 of the Doctrine and Covenants. I had never read it for myself, although I had often heard people quote from that section. When I read the three sections I was impressed that I should never drink coffee again. I simply said—to whom I did not know—"I won't ever drink coffee again," and I put my little percolator away and never drank coffee again.

Later that day I went to my office at school, closed the door, locked it, turned out the lights, and knelt down to pray. I don't know what I expected, but I did expect something—and nothing happened. I stayed there for a long time. I had no witness, no sign, no manifestation that the Church was true, so I left, saying to myself, "I'll simply forget about the Church." The problem was, I couldn't. I kept reading and thinking about it, and when I returned from Christmas vacation, I came back with the resolve to do two things: first, to go to the bishop and ask if someone could teach me more about the gospel or at least answer some of my questions, and second, to begin paying tithing.

Two men in the ward for whom I had great respect taught me every week. They didn't follow a set of lessons, but told me later they taught what they felt impressed to teach. Almost without exception it was something about which I had thought during the week prior to their teaching.

I later wrote in my journal: "I vividly recall sitting in a sacrament meeting in February. I heard little that was said in that meeting, for throughout the time the following kept running through my mind, 'Know that Joseph Smith was truly a prophet of God. Know that the Book of Mormon is the word of God. Know that my Church has been reestablished in these latter days. Know that I intend for you to be baptized. Know, believe, do.'" These words were impossible to erase from my mind, and I found it difficult in the week ahead to concentrate on anything else. The next Sunday as I passed the tray of bread to the person beside me, these words came to my mind, as surely as if a voice had spoken directly to me: "How much longer can you pass by the bread of life?" I knew where those thoughts had come from, and I knew that I did know of the truthfulness of the Church. The following Saturday, March 6, 1971, I became a member of The Church of Jesus Christ of Latter-day Saints.

In retrospect, I learned some important lessons about the Light of Christ and about the kind of influence it can be in our lives. I think now of waiting to experience some kind of sign or manifestation and compare that expectation with what we know about listening to the still small voice, which "whispereth through and pierceth all things." (D&C 85:6.) Helaman says that "it was not a voice of thunder, neither was it a voice of a great tumultuous noise, but behold, it was a still voice of perfect mildness, as if it had been a whisper, and it did pierce even to the very soul." (Helaman 5:30.)

I believe the Lord brings inspiration to our minds. I feel that the kinds of things I recorded and felt directed to do were evidences of that still small voice, of what is called the Light of Christ. In the secular world we talk about it as being our conscience—that which guides us to know good from bad, right from wrong. It is a gift given to all people that ultimately allows us to be led to know of the truthfulness of The Church of Jesus Christ of Latter-day Saints. Then, as we become baptized members, we are given the gift of the Holy Ghost, which is much more than the Light of Christ. Elder Bruce R. McConkie suggests that the companionship of the Holy Ghost is the greatest gift mortal man can enjoy. The scriptures tell us that the Holy Ghost is a teacher sent from our Heavenly Father to reveal all things necessary for the advancement of our souls, and if we think of it in that context, no wonder it is the greatest gift we can receive as mortals. Through the gift of the Holy Ghost, we can receive personal prophecy and revelation. By that gift, our minds are enlightened and ennobled, our intellect quickened, our souls purified and sanctified. By the gift and power of the Holy Ghost we are incited to do good works.

Of the things that I have read about the gift of the Holy Ghost, one of the most insightful has been what Parley P. Pratt wrote: "The gift of the Holy Ghost adapts itself to all . . . organs and attributes. It quickens all the intellectual faculties, increases, enlarges, expands, and purifies all natural passions and affections and adapts them, by the gift of wisdom, to their lawful use. It inspires, develops, cultivates, and matures all the fine-toned sympathies, joys, tastes, kindred feelings, and affections of our nature. It inspires virtue, kindness, goodness, tenderness, gentleness, and charity. It develops beauty of person, form, and features. It tends to health, vigor, animation, and social feeling. It invigorates all the faculties of the physical and intellectual man. It strengthens and gives tonic and tone to the nerves. In short, it is, as it were, marrow to the bone, joy to the heart, light to the eyes, music to the ears, and life to the whole being. In the presence of such persons, one feels to enjoy the light of their countenances, as the gentle rays of a sunbeam." (*Key to the Science of Theology*, Deseret Book, 1978, p. 61.) No wonder we need to seek for and desire to have the gift of the Holy Ghost operate in our lives.

I have always been fascinated by the ordinance of confirmation. The one being confirmed is told, "Receive the Holy Ghost." This suggests action on our part; that we do need to reach out and receive. It also implies a gift given to us, a powerful gift. Dr. David H. Yarn, Jr., suggests that "those words are addressed to us as a charge or responsibility to so conduct our lives and open our hearts to righteousness that we might be worthy to have the Holy Ghost come unto us. From that moment we had the right to receive the Holy Ghost, but he comes to us only as we manifest to God our desire and readiness to receive him in our lives." Then Dr. Yarn shares the metaphor in Revelation where Christ stands at the door and knocks. If anyone hears, let him open the door and invite the Savior in. Dr. Yarn adds, "How different is Satan and his unholy influence! He takes advantage of every opportunity to force his way into any and every nook and cranny of one's thoughts and life. In contrast, the Lord is a 'gentleman' in the most exalted sense of the word. He does not force His way into our lives. As a gentleman he stands at the door and knocks. He wants us to invite him in. If we will not get up and remove the latch and open the door, the very least we can do is ask him to enter." Then Brother Yarn makes this closing statement: "Needless to say, we should be down on our knees, pouring out our hearts and begging him to come into us." ("Discovering the Holy Ghost," *Ensign*, September 1975, pp. 71-72.)

I believe that receiving the guidance of the Holy Ghost in our lives is dependent on more than just asking for it, although certainly that is prerequisite. To seek the companionship of a member of the Godhead also requires prayers of faith and that we keep the commandments. Another clue is provided for us in Alma 17, where we are told that the sons of Mosiah fasted much and prayed much that the Lord would grant a portion of His Spirit to go with them, that they might be instruments in the hands of God. Compare that to wanting to be righteous women in the winding-up scenes before the second coming of the Savior—to literally be used by the Lord as He would see fit.

Elder Neal A. Maxwell suggests some other criteria. "We clearly cannot have the Spirit," he says, "if our lives do not reflect reasonable righteousness. We should, therefore, using the criteria given by the Lord, want to avoid trying to cover up sins, gratifying our pride and advancing our vain ambitions, or exercising compulsion over others. We should want to live in such a way that our way of living reflects relationships with others that are filled with persuasion, long-suffering, gentleness, meekness, love unfeigned, kindness and pure knowledge." (*All These Things Shall Give Thee Experience,* Deseret Book, 1979, pp. 95-96.)

For me, another way of evaluating reasonable righteousness is found in the hard questions posed in Alma 5: "Can ye look up to God at that day with a pure heart and clean hands?" "Can ye think of being saved when ye have yielded yourselves to become subjects to the devil?" "Have ye walked, keeping yourselves blameless before God? Could ye say, if ye were called to die at this time, within yourselves, that ye have been sufficiently humble?" "Behold, are ye stripped of pride?" "Is there one among you who is not stripped of envy?" Then Alma warns, "Wo unto such an one, for he is not prepared, and the time is at hand that he must repent or he cannot be saved! Repent, and I will receive you." This is a powerful guide as we seek to become righteous women and lead lives of reasonable righteousness.

I believe that living by the Spirit also requires constant effort. It is not something we work hard at and then achieve for all time. For example, one cannot go on a week-long fast and then say, "I have reached a spiritual high, it was wonderful,

and I'll have it forever and ever." It did not work that way for
the Israelites who were given manna. They were told that they
could gather manna sufficient only for one day. They couldn't
gather up enough to last them for a week; it was a daily re-
quirement. I believe spirituality is the same in our own lives: it
requires daily effort. It also requires time and practice. It
means acting when we feel impressed to—not in big, grand,
glorious ways, but responding to small impressions that come:
perhaps to visit someone who is sick, or write a note to a friend,
or make a phone call to someone in need, or put our arm
around someone who might be hurting. Learning to live by
the Spirit also suggests that we need to expect that we can receive inspiration.

Any discussion about being in tune with the Holy Ghost,
would be incomplete without at least mentioning what Dr.
Truman G. Madsen calls "spiritual deserts" or "dry spells"—
times in our lives when the Spirit withdraws and we are left to
our own judgment. I have come to believe that this is not due
to unrighteous living or because we aren't doing certain things
in our lives, but rather that there are times when this is the will
of our Heavenly Father. There have certainly been others far
greater than us who have had similar experiences. You will remember the Prophet Joseph cried out when he was impris-
oned in Liberty Jail, "Oh, God, where art thou?" (D&C 121:1.)
Christ Himself, hanging on the cross, pleaded, "My God, my
God, why hast thou forsaken me?" (Matthew 27:46.) Brother
Madsen suggests that when the Spirit withdraws, the Lord
might be saying to us, "Prove yourself devoted even when I
leave you in the realms of solitude." (*The Highest in Us,* Bookcraft, 1978, p. 91.)

Part of our challenge is learning to be righteous at all times
and under all conditions. In my own life, I have found times of
spiritual abundance alternating with feelings of perceived
abandonment. I share this journal entry:

"Because of my experiences prior to joining the Church, I
expected that following my baptism I would experience one
big spiritual high. The past ten years have taught me that
nothing could be further from the truth. Instead I find that

mountaintop experiences are separated by deserts, even valleys. I struggle with ambiguities and contradictions. I am disturbed by discrepancies between gospel principles and practices. Often I have more questions than answers, and, like Lehi, I often feel 'encompassed about because of the temptations and sins which do so easily beset me.' However, after passing through spiritual deserts where I have struggled with difficult problems, I gain new insights and understandings and realize how finite my own vision is. I no longer equate ease and comfort with happiness and contentment, but am in the process of coming to better understand the peace and joy spoken of in the gospel. No wonder our Heavenly Father, whose knowledge is perfect, provides us with spiritual deserts as well as spiritual peaks."

The gift and power of the Holy Ghost are very real. As we seek to become righteous women, to be and to share and to do our part in the building up the kingdom both numerically and spiritually in these latter days—the winding-up scenes before the second coming of the Savior—it is important that we strive to live lives that do reflect reasonable righteousness. I believe we will be blessed and strengthened by the Holy Ghost, which will permit us to do things beyond our natural abilities. The gift and power of the Holy Ghost can, indeed, make us instruments in the hands of the Lord.

Carolyn J. Rasmus is executive assistant to the president of Brigham Young University. She received her bachelor of science and master of education from Bowling Green State University and doctor of education from BYU. She has been professor of physical education at BYU, assistant professor of physical education and chairman of elementary school physical education at Iowa State University, and a teacher in Lake Ronkonkoma, New York. Active in civic affairs, she is chairman of the Provo City Airport Board and has served as chairman of the Allocations Committee panel for United Way. In the Church she has been a gospel doctrine teacher, ward and stake Young Women's president, and Relief Society spiritual living teacher.

All Thy Children Shall Be Taught

Dwan J. Young

As parents, we have the responsibility to teach our children the gospel of Jesus Christ. The scriptures are full of this admonition, and the leaders of the Church have instructed us the same way.

Heber J. Grant, the seventh president of the Church, bore a strong testimony concerning the teaching of children. He said, "The Lord has said it is our duty to teach our children in their youth, and I prefer to take His word for it rather than the words of those who are not obeying His commandments. It is folly to imagine that our children will grow up with a knowledge of the gospel without teaching. Some men and women argue, 'Well, I'm a Latter-day Saint, and we were married in the temple, and were sealed over the altar by one having the Priesthood of God, according to the new and everlasting covenant, and our children are bound to grow up and be good Latter-day Saints; they cannot help it; it is born in them.'" President Grant went on to say: "I have learned the multiplication tables, and so has my wife, but do you think I am big enough fool to believe that our children will be born with a knowledge of the multiplication tables? I may know that the gospel is true, and so may my wife; but I want to tell you that our children will not know the gospel is true, unless they study it and gain a testimony for themselves." (*Gospel Standards,* Salt Lake City: Improvement Era, 1969, p. 155.)

We cannot expect learning to take place without a plan and without effort on our part. Neither can we shift the responsibility to others.

President Joseph F. Smith counseled: "Teach to your children . . . in spirit and power, sustained and strengthened by personal practice. Let them see that you are earnest, and practice what you preach. Do not let your children out to specialists in these things, but teach them by your own precept and example, by your own fireside. Be a specialist yourself in the truth." (*Gospel Doctrine,* Salt Lake City: Deseret Book, 1939, p. 302.)

What do we need to do? We need to be fortified ourselves, to study and to prepare, and then we can be filled so that we can teach our children. Parents are the responsible party to teach—not the bishop, the Primary president, the home teacher, the priesthood advisor, or the seminary instructor. They can help supplement, but we must teach the principles.

As parents, we also appreciate the support and the help of grandparents, of other members of the family, and of loving friends, but they can only assist us. It is in a gospel-centered home, with father and mother setting the example, that family members grow in faith, centering their lives in Christ and on His teachings.

Our children today are being bombarded with philosophies and ideologies that are contrary to the plan of our Savior. With the most sophisticated technology, the media present good and bad alike, in full color with orchestra accompaniment. Elder Boyd K. Packer, in his book *Teach Ye Diligently*, states, "Many agencies are clamoring for the attention of our members, young and old alike. Providentially, most of these agencies are good and will perhaps contribute much to our teaching. However, some of them are unspeakably perverse, and their influence must be continually erased. The teaching we do must be so indelible, effective, and impressive that it cannot be erased. Then if it is covered over temporarily by falsehoods or wickedness, a good scrubbing will still leave our work intact and perhaps even a little brighter. We must teach and teach well, and teach permanently." (Salt Lake City: Deseret Book, 1977, p. 9.)

The Church recently completed a study directed specifically to young men to prepare them to be worthy and to accept mission calls. This study found that, in spite of the excellent teachers that the Church provides, and in spite of the wonderful programs that we spend so much time giving to our youth, parents still have the greatest impact on the boy. This force for good *or* bad—for the influence can either be in the right direction or in the wrong—is the strongest influence on the moral and spiritual values of the child. Interestingly, a similar study was conducted among those who are concerned with how Jewish youth develop their religious beliefs. This is what they found: Chronologically, the home is the first environment where the child experiences religion. He does not enter school until age six or seven and does not join the synagogue youth organization until his teens. What his parents do and say determine what the attitude of the teenager will be. It had been assumed that temple (or primary) schooling is sufficient, if not a necessary way to instill Jewish values into the child. Results of the study showed that this is not the case. Religious belief systems are formed at home. If one wants to affect the values of the child, he must first affect those of the parents whereby they become active in the religious education of the child. Home environment is the only variable that has any real effect upon religious beliefs and practices. ("Beliefs and Religious Practices Among Conservative Jewish Adolescents," *Adolescence* 15 [1980]: 361-74.)

Isn't it interesting that both studies happening at virtually the same time found almost identical conclusions?

Some time ago I read an article written by Dr. Elliott Landau, a professor of child development at the University of Utah. ("Children Tend to Learn Parents' Values," *Deseret*

News, November 27, 1980.) Dr. Landau quoted two Scottish psychologists who had conducted research on how children develop their moral values. The psychiatrists said, "The apple may fall far from the tree, but it doesn't often become a pear." Researchers have found that adults whom children admire make a greater impact on the social attitudes of youth than do their peers. When children have had good and strong experiences with adults, there is little need to reject adult values. Dr. Landau noted that as children get older, they separate themselves more and more from their parents and from other adults, which, of course, is necessary; and in so doing, they also move from the exact positions on matters that their parents assume. However, the children will not fall too far from the tree, and they certainly won't become vastly different from their parents. But teaching is not enough. There has to be love and respect between the teacher and the learner. Therefore, as parents it isn't enough for us to teach; we must (1) stick to our own values, (2) teach by example, and (3) then give kindness and love to the learner. Dr. Landau concludes: "What happens at home, especially if the kids love their parents, prevails."

Dr. Benjamin S. Bloom of the University of Chicago concluded from his research that a child has gone 50 percent of the way in organizing the thinking patterns that we call intelligence by the time he has reached age four and the next 20 percent by the age of eight. That's 70 percent by the age of eight. (*Stability and Change in Human Characteristics,* New York: John Wiley and Sons, 1964.)

Elder Neal A. Maxwell, speaking to Primary leaders at a Primary conference, added another dimension to this. He said: "The time to teach is when children are young, before they question authority, before they feel the power of peer pressure, and before they realize there is such a thing as adult hypocrisy and failure. We must begin early to teach and train." (*Primary Script* 13 (1968), no. 1, p. 2.)

Now, we are not talking about teaching reading, or social studies, or the multiplication tables. This kind of learning is accomplished by telling, drilling, and memorizing. We used this procedure in Primary when we had the children memorize the Articles of Faith. We told them, we drilled them, and then they memorized. We can assist children in learning skills such as riding a bicycle or picking up their clothes in their rooms. We do this by demonstrating, and they practice. We correct and guide, and they perfect. This is another kind of teaching. But moral values are taught in a very different way. Let me illustrate.

Suppose you know a family whose fifteen-year-old son has been arrested for stealing. The parents are honest, moral people. What happened? You might ask the parents, "What happened?" And they might say, "I can't understand it. We've always said what is right. We've always said what is wrong. We've told him what to do. We've told him what he shouldn't do." Maybe the mistake was that they were making the decisions for their child and not allowing him to take the consequences in small things in the beginning. In other words, the parents were acting as the conscience. The youth was still thinking like a child. Right was right only because the parents said so. When a decision needed to be made between whether to do what the parents had said or to do what the friends had wanted to do, the youth had no basis for making the judgment. Often we deprive our children of this opportunity and make the decisions for them.

Dr. Foster Cline, a child psychiatrist, said, "Values cannot be laid on a child like a coat of paint. They grow the way grain grows in wood, as part of the total development. As a child's value systems develop, they develop in stages. For instance, a four- or five-year-old tells the truth because lying isn't nice. It isn't until high school age that youth tell the truth because they realize they can't trust each other if you aren't honest. We all need to go through these stages, and if we progress through each stage successfully, we'll end up with a strong built-in set of morals and values." ("How Children Learn Right from Wrong," *Women's Day,* March 1977, pp. 66-68.)

Now let's look quickly at these five stages.

In the first stage a child must learn to trust. As we cuddle our babies, feed them, change their diapers, and talk with them, they begin to realize that they can trust us to care for them. This is fundamental to the child's whole sense of morality. While our babies are learning trust, they are also learning that they can't get everything they want, and sometimes, yes, we do have to say, "You cannot have that." They learn that no matter how hard they cry, they have to be left with a baby-sitter. They can cry, kick, scream, holler, and yell, but still the baby-sitter comes and mom and dad have to leave for a while. Slowly the trust that comes from instant gratification is balanced by tolerance for a certain amount of this frustration. This is a very important lesson to learn, because a child who is overgratified and underfrustrated is one who usually grows up to want immediate satisfaction of all his wishes and who can't handle the anxiety if he doesn't get it. So, beginning in this first year, a child learns how to work for what he wants, to plan ahead, and to understand the consequences of his actions.

The second stage begins at about age two. Children start to model their parents. How often have you heard a little one say what you have said, even in the very same tone of voice? My granddaughter Angela is three. Her mother, Chris, was having a particularly frustrating day; things were just not going well. For a long time Angela was very quiet. Then Chris noticed her standing by her side, and Angela looked up to her mom and said, "Mommy, are you having a rough day?" That's an expression that Chris has used with her children a lot when something distasteful or frustrating has happened. Then to hear her three-year-old use the same words—it is frightening to realize that they are listening so carefully to what we are saying. Children at this age not only say what we say, but they begin modeling what we do. They want to please, and they need opportunities to make decisions. For instance, if we want to teach a child to be unselfish, we might say, "Ryan, you don't have to let Rebecca play with your ball if you don't want to, but it would make her so happy if you would share, and you know, it makes mommy happy to see you share with your little sister." This way Ryan has the chance to exercise some judgment, and he also understands how we feel about it—that it will make us happy, and it will make his sister happy as well.

Stage three begins when a child is about three. During this period children start to decide what kinds of stimuli they prefer. We need to be sure our responses to their behavior provide a win-win situation instead of a win-lose. Let's say we are sewing. There are scissors on the table, and one of our children takes the pair of scissors. We might want to say, "Put those back on the table right now." So what happens? We win, he loses. Too often we do this, and our children get used to being on the outs with others. They begin to dislike what others like, and they get satisfaction from being contrary. They've been getting a response from us, and they begin to develop the feeling that if they do this wrong thing, then they'll get this kind of response. It would be better to say, "I'll bet you would like to use those scissors to cut, but you know, I'm sewing, and I need the scissors right here on the table." Then it is a win-win situation—both win. It's a positive response. Too often our reactions to our children's behavior are don'ts—don't touch this, don't do that, don't play there. This conditioning stifles and inhibits.

Stage four includes children from ages six to eleven. During this period they take a big step in their thinking about morals. They begin to realize that if something is not nice in one situation, it's not nice in another. In other words, if it is wrong to steal out of mother's purse at home, it is also wrong to steal candy from the store. They also begin to understand the consequences of what they do. How important it is that they learn these basic truths! Latter-day Saints know that the age of accountability is right in the center of that time, right when children are at the age of eight. In all of the stages until now, all we need to do is tell the child, "I want you to make me happy by doing what I think is best for you." But in this stage, we should say, "I want you to make yourself happy by learning the effect of everything that you do." Take, for example, a daughter who wants to wear her play shoes with her best dress to go to church on Sunday. Some mothers would say, "No, you are not going to wear those shoes to church; you're just not going to wear those shoes to church." A wise mother might say, "Your

Sunday shoes look so much better with your Sunday dress. Which pair do you think looks better to wear on this special day?" She could even put the clothes out on the bed—the play clothes, the dress, and the two pairs of shoes, and let the child look at them and make the decision. The result is that the child is directed as to how she feels about it, not how her mother feels. This is a period of law and order with rules to follow.

If our children have completed these four first stages successfully, then they have developed a strong conscience. By eleven a child is ready for the last stage: thinking for himself. He is used to taking the consequences for what he does, and he has a good understanding of cause and effect. When one of our sons was about eleven or twelve, one Sunday afternoon he announced that he wasn't going to go to church with us. My first reaction was to say, "Yes you are; of course you are." But my husband, who is much wiser than I, did not overreact and force Paul. He just said, "You have a right not to go to church. You know, sometimes I feel like not wanting to go either. Now, we're all going, and we would like you to come, but you need to decide. You realize that if you don't go, you'll be the only one home, and you also realize that when you're home, you're not to have any friends in while we're gone." Then all the rest of us continued to get ready. Pretty soon Paul was putting on his clothes. Nothing more was said, and we all got in the car and went to church together.

At about fifteen or sixteen, we can begin to say, "Do what you think is best," because all the elements of morality should be there by now—the loving and caring for each other, the desire for positive feedback, the ability to reason and think intelligently about values. At this time, we would be very wise to just offer our thoughts and our opinions, not lay down the law. We still need rules, but they need to be directed at how they affect *us* as parents or loved ones. For instance, if we hear a word from our teenager that is distasteful, we might say, "When you're in our home, you will not use that word. It is very crude, and we don't like it." We are telling how we feel about it, and our response is to that behavior.

As we understand these five stages, we'll become more skilled in helping our children learn basic moral concepts, which translate into character traits. These characteristics are the fundamental building blocks upon which a Christlike life is formed, and the scriptures help define for us those qualities we must develop in order to obtain exaltation—such qualities as humility, patience, and charity. During these crucial years, attitudes are also being modeled. We as parents can choose to approach life and its challenges in a positive, cheerful way. If not, we'll likely set a negative example for those about us. Such patterns become habits, and they are very difficult to break.

Let's talk now about some specific things we should teach our children in our homes. In Primary, our children sing, "Teach me to walk in the light of his love,/Teach me to pray to my Father above,/Teach me to know of the things that are right,/Teach, me, teach me to walk in the light." We must respond to this invitation. One of the requests—"Teach me to pray to my Father above"—reminds me of President Kimball's experience in that wonderful book *Spencer W. Kimball.* He told about how he learned to pray as a young boy. He said that at special times his family would pray around their revolving piano stool. The father would kneel first and put his hand on the seat. The mother would cover his hand with hers, and then each of the children would in turn put a hand on top of the other, until each hand was touching. President Kimball reflects, "We felt close together on those occasions." (Salt Lake City: Bookcraft, 1977, p. 33.) He mentioned also that there were always night prayers at "Ma's knee," and the family always knelt before meals to pray. They'd turn their plates upside down, turn their chairs away from the table, and then kneel at the chairs for the blessing on the food." (Ibid., p. 31.)

President Kimball recalled that as a little boy, he and his mother walked "up the dusty road to Bishop Zundel's house." "Why are we going?" he asked. She told him it was to take the tithing eggs. "Are tithing eggs different from other eggs?" Then Sister Kimball reminded her boy how he separated one egg from ten when he gathered them. She told him why he did so—that one egg belonged to Heavenly Father, nine to them.

What a great lesson! We could strengthen our families by following the example of these outstanding parents.

Helping our children observe the Sabbath day is a challenge. I like the song that we sing in Primary: "Saturday is a special day,/It's the day we get ready for Sunday;/We clean the house and we shop at the store, so we won't have work until Monday;/We brush our clothes and we shine our shoes, and we call it the 'get-the-work-done' day;/Then we trim our nails and we shampoo our hair, so we can be ready for Sunday!" Early preparation for the Sabbath will help make it a smoother running day. We should anticipate this day with joy, with satisfaction, and with thanksgiving. What child would not want to join a celebration if he thought Sunday was a day to celebrate—and we *can* celebrate the Sabbath, not only in resting, but in worshipping. With the new meeting schedule, we're expected to make Sunday a special day. It is a time for writing in journals, for reading to the little ones, for singing hymns, for holding family councils. One father interviews each of his children individually on Sunday. They talk about plans and goals and have a kind of accounting with their dad. With such good, positive planning and with a good attitude, the Sabbath day can be the best day of the week.

Monday is also a special day. In *Scouting* magazine, I read an article entitled "The Family: Is It Here to Stay?" That title attracted my attention because I wanted to see if the author thought families were here to stay. He went on to ask, "How does one create a cohesive family that is made up of friends, not just relatives? One way is to give time—quality time—to each other, and the father and the mother can lead the way." (Charles Graves, "The Family Hour," *Scouting*, November-December 1979, p. 52.) How proud I was to read on, because the author talked about our family home evening and described what we did in these experiences together.

Children in the Church today have increasing opportunities to become acquainted with the scriptures firsthand. In our new Primary manuals, four- and five-year-olds are being introduced to passages of the scriptures. Beginning at six, we expect children to bring their own copies of the standard works to Primary, because the lessons are planned around the children having their books right there.

By our example, we can teach our children the joy of service. We can encourage small acts of kindness within the family to help children experience the satisfaction that comes from making someone else happy. Making another family member's bed without that person's knowing it, shining someone's shoes, completing someone else's daily chores—these are examples of service within the home.

Another idea: I know of a family that was very concerned because the children were putting up on their walls posters of popular entertainment personalities. The parents planned a family home evening where they identified some of the great male and female leaders in the Church and in the scriptures. Then the children each selected one as an ideal, obtained a, picture, framed it, and hung it in their bedroom to replace the other pictures. This ties in beautifully with an activity day that we're suggesting for our Primaries. We're going to have a Heroes and Heroines Day, and we're going to encourage Primaries to identify great heroes and heroines who have the qualities we want to emulate.

Another family had a wonderful idea to help their children enjoy general conference. Each child was given a little homemade workbook that contained pictures of the General Authorities, with a blank page opposite each picture. As the General Authority spoke, the child would find the picture and write what he spoke about. Smaller children could draw a picture about what the General Authority was talking about. The last few pages of each book contained lists of words, such as love, service, and faith, and names of people, such as Jesus, Joseph Smith, and Brigham Young. The children, when they heard those words spoken by a conference speaker, would put a check or a sticker by the words as they heard them used.

As we make our homes gospel-centered, we must give our children opportunities to participate in ordinances and practice the principles of the gospel. As our children develop the traits of honesty and integrity, and as they are baptized and put the principles of the gospel into their lives, they are progressing and learning. These are all important, but in addition they must have the light spoken of in the song "Teach Me to Walk in the Light." What is this light? I think it is the understanding each child must have of his relationship to our Heavenly Father—that he is literally the spirit child of our Father in heaven, that Heavenly Father loves him, that Heavenly Father has a body with parts, and that Heavenly Father has passions and does care and feel and love. He needs to know that he has a Savior, Jesus Christ; that Jesus Christ did live and did die, and that He does live still; that the gospel—the gospel that Jesus Christ brought—is based on eternal laws; and that there are truths, and he needs to seek and live worthily to understand those truths and then be obedient so that he can return to live with our Father in heaven once more. Each child needs to have a testimony of the eternal plan, which will give him purpose and direction.

Each of us can have a positive effect on the children with whom we interact. We must develop the skills we have discussed and be more sensitive to their needs. Our attitudes and responses must be positive. We must practice the principles we preach, and we must do it all with love and with concern. Then we must bear testimony to the understanding we have of our purpose for being here, the great potential we have, and the capacity we have to return to our Father in heaven again. If we do this, we will help fulfill the promise given in Isaiah: "All thy children shall be taught of the Lord; and great shall be the peace of thy children." (Isaiah 54:14.)

Dwan J. Young is general president of the Primary in The Church of Jesus Christ of Latter-day Saints. She also serves on the governing board of Promised Valley Playhouse, the advisory board of the Great Salt Lake Council Boy Scouts of America, and the National Cub Scout Committee of Boy Scouts of America. A graduate of the University of Utah with a bachelor of science in elementary education, she taught in the Granite School District for two years. Her Church activities have included service on stake Young Women and Relief Society boards as well as stake and ward Primary assignments. She and her husband, Thomas Young, Jr., have six children.

A Deliberate Choice: Staying at Home

Beppie Harrison

Free agency offers us much more than a decision between good and evil: it opens before us a splendid panorama of choices between an infinite number of alternatives, many just as good as others. Only seldom do we encounter pure black or pure white. Most of the time most of us make our way through an ever-changing world of grays, trying to do the best we can. The choices are all there.

I suspect that we as women find this whole business a little intoxicating, particularly now in the last quarter of the twentieth century when all sorts of alternatives are readily available that our mothers or grandmothers would never have dreamed of. Opportunities that individual women had to spend their whole lives fighting for are there for our daughters to pluck as a matter of course. We can do anything, we can go anywhere, we can be anyone. Unfortunately, there's a catch involved. We do not appear to have developed nearly as spectacularly in generosity. For any choice we make, there is a vociferous minority determined to point out what a short-sighted choice it was, and how foolish we, in particular, are for having made it. If we go out to work, there is a legion reminding us that we are probably neglecting our children; if we stay at home, there is another legion reproaching us for having no spunk or ambition, and very likely not much brain either.

I have no desire to enter the discussion at this level. For one thing, I believe rather firmly in the principle of free agency, and who am I to say anything about somebody else's thoughtful decision? But there is something I feel very strongly about. I think that we as a society are letting our young daughters down. Those of us who deeply believe that it is important to do the raising of our children ourselves, that home is as valid a work place as any other, that we do not need to have a paycheck to give our efforts importance, are letting the advocates of a-job-for-everyone win by default.

I've listened to a lot of the go-out-or-stay-home debate, and it seems to me that all the advantages commonly cited are sort of vague and theoretical and sometimes downright patronizing. "Oh, of course it's *fine* to stay at home, if you *want* to." "It's good for a child to have the kind of one-to-one relationship he gets with his mother." "It's a good thing for society to have mothers at home—we've all heard about how many services depend on the volunteer hours they put in between and after child-raising." But I haven't heard anybody talk about how enjoyable it can be. I haven't heard anybody reassuring restless girls and young women that they don't have to be Mother Earth Incarnate to have fun with their own children, even if they do see them all day long. Nobody seems to be saying out loud that there are real advantages in spending our workday unsupervised in our own homes, vacuuming or sorting laundry or planting petunias, if that's what we feel like doing that day.

On the other hand, when it comes to citing the disadvantages of staying at home, the debate is depressingly specific. I have heard about the drudgery of keeping house, the boredom of conversing mainly with preschoolers, the feeling of being trapped by responsibilities that last for years. And I'm perfectly willing to admit that all that can be true, and even that it *is* true, some days. But I want to let all these young women, forming their ideas and looking forward to their lives, into a very well-kept secret. Nothing they can choose to do will *not* have moments of drudgery or boredom, maybe even of feeling trapped. Unfortunately, that is what much of life is all about: making the best of being bored, getting through the drudgery, finding internal freedom when our circumstances have us trapped. It all happens anywhere. It happens at home; it happens on the job: it happens simply because we're human beings in an imperfect world, surrounded by other human beings.

Maybe we've fallen into this business of viewing home as a particularly unrewarding workplace without quite realizing it. Part of it comes from the new emancipation of being able to complain about our children and our families. When I was growing up, everybody sort of expected that girls would grow up to be wives and mothers. Maybe they'd do something else before they settled down, but nobody suggested that settling down wasn't the point of the game, unless one wanted a career, which was always something special and implied a mannish suit and the willingness to plow under family considerations. A sensible woman who had found a husband and produced children kept her mouth shut about any drawbacks she found in the arrangement.

Then came women's liberation. Women's liberation suddenly freed us to complain. And complain we have, long and loud. Mind you, I'm not saying there aren't things to complain about. As a fascinating conversationalist, a two-year-old has unavoidable limitations. If there is any one thing to be said about scrubbing the kitchen floor, it is that it will have to be scrubbed again—probably tomorrow, if we have small children. Few husbands are really ready for immediate translation into glory. (Neither are very many wives, but that's not the point at the moment.) So complaining felt *good*. It was absolutely lovely to say all those things out loud that we'd been thinking and to discover that we were not alone in feeling that way. And with joy and mingled voices, our complaining rose louder and louder until all of a sudden we found ourselves seeming to say to the young girls coming up that the transitory mood of a stormy or unsettled day is The Way Life at Home Is. All the time.

Staying home with young children is, like anything else, whatever we want to make of it. But being around young children day after day has the potential for more amusement, enjoyment, and satisfaction than practically any other job going. At seventeen months, my James does not discuss current affairs with me very well, but nobody else in the world greets me with the same lovely, wholehearted grin that he does. There is one human being in the world to whom I am faultless, beautiful, the unfailing source of warmth and comfort. Talk about being good for my ego! Of course, he'll grow out of it, and I hope that as he discovers the many imperfections his sisters have already identified, he will continue to be fond of the poor old woman—but I've got that adoration now, and it gets me through a lot of dirty diapers and oatmeal painted on the furniture.

These aren't once-in-a-while moments of satisfaction. They happen all the time. And there's nothing particularly brilliant or adorable about my children, except of course to me. That's what young children are like, and it's every bit as true as the propaganda that says they are noisy, messy pests. I want the young girls who are growing up to know that.

Children are funny. We can laugh harder at—and with— our children than at any TV comedy. Sometimes it's unconscious humor; sometimes it's the family clown for the day, who is enjoying his performance as much as his spectators are. Children can make us catch our breath with amazement at their thought-provoking observations. They're busy all day long in the important work of organizing their impressions and discovering what kind of a world this is—and sometimes they put things together in a totally new and exciting way that changes the whole way we look at something from that time forward.

Children are lovable. It's when we have one of our own that we suddenly realize how much we love that scrap of humanity. Sometimes we realize it with a sweeping suddenness when we see the naked newborn in the delivery room; sometimes it happens later, when a flood of maternal possessiveness suddenly takes us by surprise. But whenever, however, it happens, it's that love that sustains us through all the weeks and months before the baby can give anything back. There's the first smile, the first real smile with the eyes as well as the crooked little mouth, but to me, the real first is the first time I feel the baby arms around my neck giving me a genuine hug. That reduces me to putty. And they go on being lovable. They're lovable when they're hot and grubby, and when they're sprawled and defenseless in sleep, and even when they're naughty. I can be legitimately and justifiably furious, and in the middle of expressing my righteous indignation I suddenly see that small stricken face staring up at me, and my heart twists with love. They are no less lovable as teenagers, elaborately nonchalant with success or heartbreakingly vulnerable when things have gone wrong. Big, little, good, bad, awake, asleep—we need a whole new vocabulary of love for our children.

Of course, none of this happens without our putting a lot of work in. But that's true of anything. I don't quite understand why work on a job for which we get paid is somehow considered more meaningful than the work we do at home, calmly, repetitively teaching that cushions belong on the couch and feet belong on the floor, that you do need to take a bath even if you did have one yesterday, that you do not snatch the train from your brother even if you do want to play with it, and most important of all, you do not, repeat, do *not* walk in muddy boots across that section of floor you can see your mother is mopping.

Some of the work we do is peculiar to the career of being a housewife—just as certain work is peculiar to being a secretary, or a computer programmer, or even a fashion model, I suppose—but a lot of the needed skills are the same ones we have to work on in any profession. Calmness, patience, a willingness to let bygones be bygones and move onto the next problem—that's just part of getting along with people. Did you ever hear of office politics? Exactly the same emotions fuel those interesting encounters with a teenager that end with a slammed bedroom door and us breathing heavily in the kitchen trying to calm down and keep our sense of proportion. In those moments it might be a comfort to think of the working women all over the country leaning on the water cooler seething with fury over the pigheadedness of boss or subordinate. People are people, wherever they are. And the big advantage to dealing with people at home is that deep down, sometimes *very* deep down, we love each other. We *care* about each other. So eventually we finish doing our deep breathing, and calmly, humbly, knock on the door and confess where we feel we lost control, and start over again on the business of trying to reach each other across the misunderstanding. And when we've crossed it at last, we've gotten a lot further than that woman at the water cooler. With the same reconciliation effort, she may have burnished her image with her boss, or guaranteed more productive time from her underling, but we've helped strengthen links that are going to last through eternity. That is love, and I think I'm immensely fortunate to have it a part of my daily working life.

There is one infallible method for getting oneself into this career of being a housewife. A young woman meets some personable young man and marries him, and one things leads to another, and there she is, newly retired from the working world, very probably because she's expecting her baby in a month or so. She has become a Housewife.

That is what happened to me—not exactly when, as a young girl, I might have expected it to happen. But the Lord moves in mysterious ways. As a parent now, I find it fascinating to consider the way in which the Lord tailors the life experiences of each of his multitudinous children here on earth to provide each of us with exactly the learning experiences we need and can grow upon. Obviously perfectly aware that this particular daughter has a stubborn and argumentative streak, the Lord has had a pattern for me that has consistently been to withhold a blessing until I have really realized that down to the very foundation of my soul, that is what I have wanted. So it was with my marriage.

During the years when most of my friends were meeting and marrying, I was meeting and not marrying. It was never right. The young men who wanted to marry me were nice people but never more, and the young men I wanted to marry clearly preferred to wait for someone else. So, by default more than by design, I developed a career. I had the satisfaction of discovering that there was work I could do well; I had the independence of being able to decide what I wanted to do, how I should spend my money, where I thought it would be nice to go; and gradually, day by day, month by month, year by year, I learned that for me, that wasn't enough. I looked at my friends who were flourishing and floundering in early marriage, starting families with budgets stretched beyond the breaking point, and did my best not to envy their struggles. But I knew, ever more surely, that their battlefield was the one I wanted to fight on. So when, late in my twenties, I encountered a particularly fascinating young British architect, I realized immediately that not only did I very much want to marry *him*—I very much wanted to *be* married.

Now, fifteen years later, I still feel exactly the same way. Of course, in the way we each tend to think our personal experience has universal application, I believe there is a great deal to be said for a young woman's giving herself a chance to grow up and find out who she is before hurling herself into matrimony and a new family. On the other hand, my sister, who lives near me with her seven children and her husband whom she married when she was nineteen, believes equally firmly that she married at exactly the right time for her, and that the struggles to grow up together have welded them into an extraordinarily close and intimate unit. So I guess there is no generally applicable formula, and the best we can say to every young woman is be as wise as she can, pray honestly, and be prepared to find answers in ways she may not expect. Most of all, she should be careful. Her marriage is the foundation and cornerstone of her family for now and forever, and eternity is a very long time to spend with the wrong person. Of all the reasons there are for marrying, there is only one that I can say unequivocably is a bad one, and that is to marry because one's best friend is marrying.

After the marriage come the children. Right then is when the woman of today has to make her decision. It didn't used to be such a visible fork in the road. For most women, the choice was automatic. You had children and you stayed home with them. But women's liberation, which has made so many alternatives available to us, has produced a climate of opinion in which the choice to stay at home and raise your children yourself is simply another one of those alternatives; and, if we're to be absolutely honest about the general attitude of today, rather a shabby and unimaginative alternative at that.

There is no doubt that for many mothers, the choice to stay at home with their children does not exist. The quality of mothering done by many of those women who have to split themselves between two lives reduces me to humble admiration. But I am not talking about them. I am talking about the rest of us, women who may dress less elegantly and eat more macaroni and cheese on a single income than we would with two paychecks coming in, but who basically have the option to choose not to sell their time. Surrounded by loud praise of the independence and self-fulfillment of the wage earner, and tempted by the thousands of delightful goodies we could have so much more easily if there were more money flowing into the family coffers, we Latter-day Saint women sometimes feel we are alone in being counseled to stay at home with our growing children. We're not. Ruth Graham, the wife of the Reverend Billy Graham, has said that the real liberation of women would be to be freed from the burden of working outside the home. She goes on to say that where there is genuine economic necessity, the children recognize it. "Children are perceptive," she says. "They know if their mother is working for an extra color television or because the family cannot do without the money she earns."

So if by choosing not to work outside the home we are also choosing not to have that extra color television for our children (and most of us on a single income in these hard times are making that kind of choice), and given that staying at home has very positive and enjoyable aspects for us as individuals, what do the kids get out of it?

One of the biggest things, I would suggest, is that much maligned *quantity* time that the trendy ladies dismiss so cavalierly. You know the line: "Oh, but I have *quality* time with my children." Well, I have quantity time, and I would bravely suggest that it's every bit as important. I think that children learn a lot of what it is to be an adult during the times when nobody is paying any particular attention to them. I would even hint that the child whose mother focuses her whole attention upon that child whenever they are together is developing a distorted idea of what a woman's life is all about.

I contend that my children are learning constantly, and valuable lessons at that. We are encouraged to keep our houses and yards in order. And how is this tidiness supposed to happen? Little as they are, my children learn that a neat and tidy home is not created by waving a wand. They learn that it takes work, that playthings as well as grown-up possessions have places where they belong, that spilled juice has to be mopped up by somebody, and that dirty clothes have to be physically moved from the spot where they are discarded to get into the laundry. Apparently these are not easy lessons to learn, judging by the daily necessity to teach them all over again, but I am convinced that the baby trotting after me as I vacuum is gradually developing a preference for cleanliness.

I honestly don't feel I need to be apologetic about spending time on the telephone sharing confidences with a friend while Marianna hangs on my leg begging for attention. She'll get her attention when I hang up. Since I'm home all day, there's time to sit down and find out what she wanted and to give her a tickle and a cuddle, interrupted only by James, who wants some too. But it hasn't hurt her to wait. She is just beginning to have friends, and somewhere in her developing world view I want her to learn that grown-ups have friends as well, and like to spend time with them. We all have a lifelong battle with jealousy in a thousand different forms. Perhaps

Marianna, competing for my attention with my friend on the phone, is on her way to learning that there is room for many friends in my life, that she herself is by far one of the most important of my friends, but not the only one.

I'm glad I have quantity time to offer my children, because their crises and problems are not synchronized with the pattern of a working day. My oldest is just approaching adolescence, but I can see already that as she grows older, problems that are urgent when they arise—generally just after school—may have faded by later in the afternoon, when a working mother is just getting home. This is not to say that a working mother can't be responsive and consoling, but it's a lot harder. It doesn't take great sensitivity to figure out something's wrong when a tear-stained face greets you at the door, but I worry that I would miss some of the very faint signals of distress I hear in the carefully controlled account she may give her father that evening when he's home. No mother can make everything all better; growing up is hard. But at least I'm there to offer comfort and companionship, even if my mind is sometimes distracted.

Our children need to learn about independence and self-reliance, even in such simple ways as learning to amuse themselves. In a way, the child whose mother feels obliged to be a constant entertainment director is as crippled as the child who spends hours mesmerized by the television screen. How many of us remember childhood hours lying on the grass watching clouds drift past? We are so inundated by advice these days on how to challenge a child's intelligence that we sometimes forget that children need time to discover what they want to learn, and that a child may long as much as we do for a moment when there is nothing to do next—when he can, if he wishes, do nothing for a few minutes. Even the daughter hanging on our chair and whining, "I'm bored," is, after all, just one more in the long chain of generations of children complaining of boredom, and if we are in the middle of making up a grocery list, or mending some trousers, or writing a letter, or even reading the comics, there is no reason in this world why she can't wait until we are finished—by which time, in the exasperating way of children, she will probably have thought up something absolutely fascinating all by herself.

There are certainly times when we want to share their activities, but those are not all of the times. In the quantity of time we have together, there are hours to spend jointly and hours to spend separately.

As women in the Church, we have special responsibilities to teach our children how the gospel forms the pattern and structure of our daily life. All that time on the telephone pinning down a substitute to teach our Primary class is one way a child, overhearing, learns that we have the responsibility for working out the administration of the Church here on earth. The child hanging around as his mother arranges for dinners to be brought in for a mother with a new baby, or sets up appointments for her visiting teaching, is learning something about compassionate service and the sturdy network of sisterhood in the Church. The child listening to us passing on the special request for ward members to fast and pray for a family in particular difficulties is learning about faith and the love we try to share with one another.

The temptation to reserve scripture reading for times when the children are peacefully in bed is enormous, and yet our children need to see us reading the scriptures for our own spiritual development. They need us to read the scriptures to them, but they also need to see that we as their mothers read the scriptures for ourselves, not simply as a good example, but as food for our spirits as vital as the food we place on the dining room table for our bodies. The child watching his mother reading the scriptures with an absorption so total she doesn't even notice he is there is learning a lesson as important as many she will teach with her full attention to him. These are quantity time lessons that nobody else can teach our children, because to a child his mother is somebody utterly separate from all the others. To see the part the gospel plays in his mother's life has a significance it would not have if it were, for example, a babysitter doing exactly the same thing.

The gospel gives us the entirely unique perspective of seeing our families as eternally joined. I have lots of friends. Some I enjoy for one reason, some for another. We share different facets of this amazing world. But of all my friends, the two whose relationship with me matters the most are my two sisters, because we are the only ones who have this eternal dimension to our friendship. It amplifies the giggles and sharing; it makes struggling through the arguments and irritations an absolute necessity; it locks us together in cozy warmth. We're going to be bumping up against each other for a long, long time. And so when I look at my own squirming, brawling, all too frequently squabbling brood, I am determined to do everything I can to help them develop the same strong bonds between them that will last when time itself has lost its meaning. I don't know how others make brothers and sisters love each other, but I suspect a most important aspect is to keep down as much as possible the obstacles to their discovering that love all by themselves. Trying to be as fair as possible and yet letting each of them know that each is different and therefore gets my love and attention meted out in slightly different ways—that can't be equalized like apples or oranges. I try to seize upon each demonstration of respect and affection they give each other, and lavish upon them praise and appreciation, letting them know that these are the attitudes I value, the virtues I encourage. I also believe in insisting that however heated the sisterly (or brotherly) debate, it is to be conducted in a civil tone of voice and to take into consideration the probability that the erring sibling did whatever she did for motives that seemed reasonable to her at the time. In other words, the children should learn to treat their sisters and brothers as they would treat their friends, because for all the long years and yearless span ahead, their siblings are going to be their friends—their cherished, infuriating, eternal friends.

Now, I certainly do not wish to imply that any of these values and lessons are mystic secrets, beyond the grasp of any woman who chooses to work outside her home. Other women make other choices, and many of them find time for a range of housekeeping and mothering activities quite apart from their wage-earning duties. All I really know about is me, and I know

I have a definitely finite amount of time and energy available. I am grateful that I have the opportunity to spend most of both in the place and with the people who matter most of all to me. My children will outgrow me, as I have outgrown my mother; the absolute dependency of the infant gradually ebbs and dwindles away and is replaced by the friendship of two adults who know each other with the greatest possible intimacy. This time with them close to me is so short, I want to cry out. I cannot bind them close to me; I can only nurture and treasure the love we have for each other, which will join us when the elemental need is gone. Time passes, and as it passes, the bodies of my children grow to match their spirits, which were never younger than mine. This time when they are entrusted into my care is only an interval, after all.

In this swirling sea of change there is only one other fixed point, my husband. Poor invisible man: I've hardly mentioned him, intent as I have been on the elements of my working day, when he is away at his office. And yet he plays an enormous part in my life. I think the interplay and balance between working husband and stay-at-home wife is particularly important and often misjudged and maligned. My husband is my window on the world. During these years of intensive child-rearing, his orbit is obviously much wider than mine. He is out in the world every day; I take periodic forays, frequently with children clutching my skirts. Our roles are interlaced. If for me he represents a fresh breeze from outside, for him I am a haven from competition, someone whose love and respect are not related to his level of achievement. What we need from each other, what we do for each other, is different. This is not to say that there are not times when he is amused and refreshed by a glimpse of the different world I inhabit, times when he is the haven for me from the frustrations and exasperations of dealing with our children. And sometimes our needs to receive comfort and reassurance coincide on the same days, and there is a brief brisk struggle to determine who is going to be the haven for whom. Perhaps the most important thing is that we see our accomplishments and achievements as shared. We both glow with pride when our daughter performs the piano sonata, practice for which I have supervised for weeks on end; and we are both triumphant when his architectural work receives an award.

I truly don't understand why my sense of achievement in these accomplishments should be denigrated, as it often is. I have heard people say bitterly that women like me are only finding ourselves through others, instead of doing anything on our own. Don't they understand the concept of working on joint endeavors? Is the lighting director to take no pride in what he does because he is not the actor on the stage? Has the producer no creative function because his work is done away from the audience? I am sure my husband would do well if I were not there; I know he does better because I am, and in my opinion this fact diminishes neither of us. A human being, I believe, is built to lean just a little—to lean upon a loved partner, to lean upon the Lord.

Like the Lord, my husband knows all about me and loves me anyway. My baby, James, thinks I am wonderful and marvelous and all-powerful because he is young and ignorant. In time he will grow up and find out about me; and eventually, I hope, he will find some young woman who will do some things differently and some things the same, and he will come to love her the way my husband loves me—strengths, weaknesses, and all. In return I hope he, and the girls, will come to know the uniquely rewarding territory of marriage, the closeness, the sharing, the wordless communication across the room, the jokes nobody else would understand or care about. It won't be good all the time; no marriage is good all the time. My bishop counseled us wisely when we were married. He told us we need love most when we deserve it least. And we need the love of the Lord. I am so grateful for the Church, for the framework it gives to the fabric of my life, for the discipline, the authority, the strength, and the promises.

Sometimes I can shut my eyes and almost feel the golden days slipping away, as babies scramble into toddlers, and toddlers lengthen into schoolchildren, and childhood blurs into adolescence. These years are so very short, and there's the whole world out there waiting for me when they are gone. I think of those young girls of today, surrounded by the subtle and not-so-subtle urgings to turn their backs on the traditional roles of women, and I want to tell them with all my heart: think carefully. Pray hard, and listen very, very intently for your particular guidance. I can't tell them what it will be. But I can tell them that that lifework of being a wife and mother is one of the most joyous, most demanding, most satisfying opportunities that exists, and I am passionately grateful that that lifework is mine.

Beppie Harrison received a bachelor's degree from the University of California at Berkeley. Her editorial experience has included stints as an editor at the University of California Press, production editor for Doubleday, and executive project coordinator and consultant for a London book publisher. A free-lance writer, she is the author of a book titled Mysterious Regions (1978) and co-author of Giving Time a Chance (1983). She is currently working on a book about parenting. In the Church she has been a ward Primary president and counselor in a ward Relief Society. Her civic activities include service as a Brownie co-leader and as a leader in the Junior Great Books program. She and her husband, Geoffrey Harrison, have four children; they reside in Birmingham, Michigan.

Making You
and Your Child
Successful

Claudia Fuhriman Eliason

A balloonist was selling balloons on the streets of New York. He had white balloons, red balloons, yellow balloons, and brown balloons. Every once in a while he would let one go, and as it would sail through the sky, children from blocks around would come to him to buy his balloons. One little black boy came up and tugged at his arm and said, "Sir, if you had a black balloon, would it go up too?" The wise balloonist looked at the little lad and said, "Son, it's not the color of the balloon that sends it up, it's what's inside that sends it up." (Zig Zigler, *See You at the Top,* Gretna, La.: Pelican Publishing Company, p. 41.)

Within every one of us are two things that send us up. One is a testimony of the gospel of Jesus Christ, and the other is self-esteem—the assurance that "I am okay, I am worthwhile."

A testimony can bring peace, joy, and assurance. It should also bring self-respect, for at the very heart and core of each of our testimonies should be that sure knowledge that we are literally sons and daughters of our Heavenly Father, each of us a child of God. As members of the Church, then, that knowledge should bring us self-esteem and a feeling of self-worth. It should bring dignity and respect, because among all the peoples of the world, we know who we are, whence we have come, and why we are here. To those of us who are building self-esteem, gaining a testimony should be the first stepping-stone, the foundation stone that we work on. For those of us working on it or as parents helping children develop it, let's start at that point then—teaching them that they are literally important children of a Father in heaven who loves them, who reveres them, who respects them, who hopes for them. This should be the basic building block of our self-esteem.

Self-esteem is the courage to take risks, to stand up and defend that which we believe in. It is a feeling of adequacy and worth. It marks us for success or failure in life, for we are what we think we are, and we can become only that which we think we can become. It means accepting ourselves and our strengths as well as our limitations, viewing both our strengths and our limitations realistically.

We should read often Doctrine and Covenants 46:11: "All have not every gift given unto them; for there are many gifts, and to every man is given a gift by the Spirit of God." What a promise that is for us, and especially each of our children. We may not have everything, but Heavenly Father has promised that we each have at least one special gift that we can develop and share with others, and we may even have many gifts. In addition, we have been told that we have weaknesses, and we are told why we have weaknesses: "If men come unto me I will show unto them their weakness. I give unto men weakness that they may be humble; and my grace is sufficient for all men that humble themselves before me; for if they humble themselves before me, and have faith in me, then will I make weak things become strong unto them." (Ether 12:27.) If we humble ourselves before our Father in heaven and before our brothers and sisters, recognizing our weaknesses and that we may not be good in all things, He will help us work on what we have as we strive for perfection.

Those who have self-esteem do not usually have a strong need for recognition and approval, because that is intrinsically within them. They *know* they have worth. They don't have to have people constantly telling them that they are great, although deserved praise should certainly be given. Little children, as they are developing their self-concepts, need this constant reassurance. Even many adults are still struggling with self-esteem, and they also need all of the honest praise, approval, and recognition that we can give them.

Some wonder if self-esteem isn't really conceit; however, it is the opposite of conceit. The person who is conceited and tries constantly to prove his worth to others often has an underlying low self-esteem that really needs building. A person with low self-esteem may also seek to criticize and tear others down in hopes of raising his own esteem. A person with self-esteem does not need to prove his worth or excellence to others. He does not need constant praise and credit in order to feel good about himself, because he has a genuine feeling of worth within; in addition, he can feel genuinely good about another's good fortune, achievement, success. When we reach the point where we can go to another's home and share with genuine delight the things he has and feel as good for him as we would for ourselves, then we have achieved the kind of self-actualization and esteem that I would hope we would all work toward. A person with self-esteem feels neither inferior nor superior to others.

Self-esteem is woven into a child's personality from threads of constructive experiences and from the warm and loving approval of people with whom he associates, particularly his parents. As a child's self-esteem grows, initially he is greatly influenced by the way others view him. This is called mirror image, the tendency to see ourselves as we think others see us. As adults, we need to constantly provide positive and realistic mirror images for children, because they are relying upon us to help them find out how to view themselves. Self-esteem brings confidence—confidence to step out and do the things that Heavenly Father expects us to do. But it takes confidence and self-esteem to do all that is expected and to reach our potential. Let me share with you an experience that illustrates this.

At Utah State University I had the opportunity of teaching young children three to five years of age and training teachers in the preschool labs. On the last day of little Timothy's experience in the lab, I said, "Oh, Timothy, I'm going to miss you." He shrugged his shoulders and said, "It's okay, I'll see you in heaven." I thought, *That's confidence, isn't it!*

We must believe in ourselves before we can believe in, strengthen, help, and accept others. As mothers, grandmothers, and teachers, let us work on building our own self-esteem and examine our own souls to find out where we are. It is difficult to build and strengthen others if we don't have self-esteem, because we are consumed with criticizing, defending, and worrying about our own selves. It is so much easier to lose ourselves in serving others when we feel good about ourselves. Through growth and maturity and many positive experiences, we may reach a point of self-actualization, of having self-esteem. Then, because we are not tied up with our own selves, we can literally lose ourselves in the service of others—our children, our grandchildren, our neighbors next door, across town, or around the corner, those in need. To me, then, the serving, the lifting, the acts of charity are what I think we mean by "charity never faileth." This kind of charity or service does not fail those whom we serve, and it never fails those who are giving service. It only lifts us up. I believe this is what the Savior meant when He said, "He that loseth his life for my sake shall find it." (Matthew 10:39.)

I would like to suggest some foundation stones and then some specific stepping-stones leading toward self-esteem. They can be applied to ourselves as well as to those whom we serve, particularly our children.

The first foundation stone is love. This is absolutely vital. Every single person needs to know that he or she is truly loved. Without love, self-esteem is very, very difficult. Love is like a welcome rain shower, for it lifts the drooping and it heals. Feelings of love are caught and not taught. Yes, we can say to the child, "I love you," but he needs to feel it from expressions in our eyes, from having his hair ruffled, from that little squeeze we give him as we pass, from spontaneous responses both vocally and physically.

The second foundation stone is time. I love what I call the "Mormon commercials." I love the phrase, "Give your children everything. Give them your time." Giving time says to a child, "I love you." Giving time says, "You have worth, you are important." A poem many years ago in the *Instructor,* titled "Dad," told about a little boy who went into his father's workshop, climbed up on his knee, and said, "I wish my daddy was a dog." His father asked why, and he said, "Because dogs always have time. They never say, 'Don't get in the way.'" The poet said that was one of the most precious times of his life, when he realized that his little boy needed his time. He concluded:

> *I find the richest entry*
> *Recorded in this daily log*
> *Is the day that small boy whispered,*
> *"I wish my Daddy was a dog."*[1]

The third foundation stone is patience. When I was teaching students, I used to talk a lot about love and about time—and I didn't know about patience. Now, with six little ones, I know how important patience is. At times when the milk is spilled, or at five or six o'clock when everyone is tired and hungry—those are the times when we need to work on patience a little more. Children know more of our love when they are assured of our patience. I think that many times we say, "I love you," but because we are so impatient with their mistakes and imperfections, they assume that we don't love them. Patience says, "I love you."

With these three general foundation stones, then, let us look at some specific stepping-stones or techniques.

1. Help our children set and accomplish goals. President Spencer W. Kimball reportedly has a sign on his desk that says,

---

[1]Elwood C. Leany, quoted in Calvin C. Cook, "And the Glory of Children Are Their Fathers," *Instructor,* May 1966, pp. 94-95.

"Do it." We need to teach children to act upon and do something about the resolutions they make. We need to do that ourselves. We need to chart our course by setting realistic goals, and also to help our children become goal oriented. Accomplishment of goals brings self-worth within. We need to learn to do it *now.* The story of Jesus calling His first disciples, Simon and Andrew, is a wonderful example of doing it now. They were fishermen, and the scriptures tell us that they left their nets *straightway.* Wouldn't it have been easy for them to say, "Oh, yes, I'll follow, but wait until after the fishing season," or "Let me just catch fish the rest of the day," or "Wait until next week"? Rather, they left their nets immediately. Let us learn to work on our goals now, and as we accomplish each one, we can move on to other things. This brings feelings of self-esteem and self-worth.

2. Set an example for them by smiling. As parents, as neighbors, as friends, we need to be a smiling people, positive and happy. I have a friend who has taught me much. She has nine children, and one day, as she was busily getting them off to school and to their jobs, her youngest, Christopher, asked, "Mommy, who's coming today?" She said, "No one that I know of. Why do you ask?" And he said, "Because you have your other-people's face on." She told me in shock, "I realized I'd been smiling that morning." Then she added, "From now on, I'm going to look first thing in the morning and see if I have my other-people's face on." Shouldn't we smile and be happier and more friendly with our family members than with anyone else? Unfortunately, we sometimes show less respect for those we love the most. We need to think and act positively. We break down feelings of self-worth when we are negative. Too often parents notice the negative things children do instead of the positive things.

3. Do kind deeds, the little acts that let them know we think they are important. For example, when a mother is fixing dinner, she might think, "I know that Suzanne loves strawberry gelatin with bananas in it; I'm going to fix it for her." Then, as she serves that dinner she might say to the family, "We're having this because I know it is Suzanne's favorite dish." We

should let our children know that we are sensitive to their likes and their dislikes and their feelings. Kind deeds make such a difference.

We must learn to accept children's little gifts and deeds as well as giving to them. When I was teaching first grade, a little boy came to my desk one day not long after Thanksgiving and said, "Miss Fuhriman, I've got a gift for you." He handed me a crumpled brown paper bag, and as I opened it, I found twenty-three turkey wishbones. (I guess he had gone to all the neighbors and collected them for me.) I said, "That is one of the most special gifts I have ever received. I'll have twenty-three wishes." And each day he came and asked, "Did you make a wish?" I said, "I surely did." Accepting children's little gifts says "I accept you."

4. Accept their individual differences. I believe that nothing is so unequal as equal treatment of unequals. Each child is different, so each must be treated differently. Each has different needs. We need to help children gear expectations for themselves that are right for them. Expecting a child to jump hurdles that are too high can only engender failure and feelings of defeat, discouragement, and low self-esteem. As adults, we too often forget this. We constantly expect too much of ourselves. We criticize ourselves. We forget to look at our strengths, and we see only our weaknesses—and they become magnified in great proportion. Too often we compare ourselves to others' best. Though standards may be high, we should not lose sight of where we are and who we are and that we need to put one foot in front of the other and work every single day. These are lessons we need to learn for ourselves and then to teach our children.

5. Help each child to recognize his strengths and to capitalize on them and share them with others. We can encourage our children to keep victory lists, maybe in the front of their journals or on a bulletin board. These are the little things each day that have gone well for them, their successes. Then, on those days when things don't go so well and they're feeling discouraged, they can turn to their victory lists. For a family home evening, we might have each person share

thoughts from his or her victory list, those tangible things that
have said, "You have achieved. You are okay. You are worthwhile." We need to learn to focus upon those rather than upon
the bad things and the not-so-good things that happen to all of
us as individuals. The stumbling block comes when we compare ourselves to others rather than to ourselves and the goals
that we have established. Let's remind our children constantly
of their strengths, their resources, their gifts, and their talents.

6. Praise them for specific efforts and accomplishments. In
fact, we might try to come up with ten or twenty or fifty ways of
saying, "You are terrific. That was a super job." Then we need
to tack that list to a bulletin board or the refrigerator and use
those phrases often. All of us need this kind of praise as we
work toward self-esteem, but children especially need it. I'm
reminded of the story of the little boy who said to his mother,
"Mother, come and play a game of darts with me." And she
said, "All right, son." As they went downstairs to the dart
board, he said, "I'll throw the darts. You say 'Wonderful, wonderful.'" We need to work on our journals together with our
children and to talk and write about their successes. We can
value their art work, their written work, and keep a scrapbook
for them with their special things.

7. Help them be content with where they are and who they
are. I like the phrase "Bloom where you're planted." Recently
my two little girls, Erin and Megan, were playing while I was
ironing, and I said to them, "Tell me something about you
that's special—the color of your hair, or something else about
yourself that you like." We took turns doing this for a while,
and suddenly Megan said, "I'm me. I'm in this skin and I like
me." I don't know exactly why she thought in those terms, but
I said, "Yes, and you are a child of God, and He loves you, and
I love you." It was a special time that just came about in conver-
sation. I think too often some adults and some children, especially teenagers, spend too much time hoping, dreaming, and
searching instead of being content with what *is* and then working on what *can be.*

8. Help them stay free from sin. This is very important to
self-esteem, for the burden of guilt breeds low self-esteem.

Elder James E. Faust has said in a conference address: "Chastity nurtures and builds feelings of self-worth and indemnifies against the destruction of self-image. . . . Can we respect ourselves when we do things that we do not admire and may even condemn in others?" (*Ensign*, May 1981, p. 9.) If a child has made mistakes, if he has done anything that is wrong, he needs to know that there is a way back through repentance. He needs to free himself again of any guilt that is too big a burden to carry around. He cannot have the kind of self-esteem and self-actualization that he is searching for when he is burdened with heavy guilt.

9. Let them do things on their own. Independence breeds self-respect, and freedom and dignity are its prizes. Sometimes it is so much easier for us to do it ourselves when children want to help with preparing dinner, when they want to sweep the floor, when they want to wash. It's so much easier to say, "No, let me do it." And even as the children are getting ready for school and their little fingers have a hard time tying shoes, it's so much easier to say, "Let me do it." If we do that throughout their lives, then they begin to think, "I can't, I can't. I have to lean on someone else." It's hard to untie the apron strings and let children handle independence as they are able. And yet, we must. We must let them do things when they are ready, let them know that they can, and help them learn how.

10. Expand their spiritual and intellectual horizons. As they learn new concepts in the scriptures, as they learn new things at home and school, they walk a little taller and they feel proud of having increased knowledge. We need to help them develop skills and competencies and encourage them to seek after knowledge, to read good books, and to study. This will bring increased self-esteem and self-worth.

11. Encourage them to serve. As they help others, they will come to know and understand themselves better. We should teach them to look beyond the masks that people wear, beyond the outside physical image, and to seek to find out what is within that person. By serving others, our children not only know others better, but they will also grow themselves.

May we always remember how important our teaching of little children is, as we remember the words so often quoted by Elder Boyd K. Packer:

> *Plastic little children,*
> *Made of Heaven's clay,*
> *Oh Father, give us vision*
> *To mold them right this day.*
>
> *Potential Gods in miniature,*
> *We must have help from Thee,*
> *For how they're fashioned here today*
> *Will endure through all eternity.*[1]

Claudia Fuhriman Eliason received her bachelor of science and master of science from Utah State University and later served as an assistant professor of family and human development at USU. She has also been director of a child-care curriculum project for the Utah State Board of Education and a visiting professor at the University of Lethbridge, Alberta, Canada, and is the author of a text titled A Practical Guide to Early Childhood Curriculum. She has appeared in Outstanding Young Women of America and World Who's Who of Women in Education. In the Church she has served as a stake Primary president, member of the Primary general board, and member of a stake Relief Society presidency. She and her husband, Dr. Glen M. Eliason, reside in Ogden, Utah. They have six children.

---

[1]Author unknown. Quoted in *Teach Ye Diligently* (Salt Lake City: Deseret Book, 1975), p. 266.

The Blessing
of Music
in the Home

Sally Peterson Brinton

Recently I once again had the privilege of participating in
God's greatest miracle—the birth of a precious new baby, a
little baby girl complete with fingers and toes, a rosy com-
plexion, a wailing cry, and a sweetness of spirit fresh from
the presence of our Father in heaven.

Oh, the emotions of overwhelming joy that flooded my
soul as I thanked my Father in heaven for the divine calling of
being a mother! As I held that little bundle in my arms for the
first time, I reflected upon the decisions along life's paths that
brought me to that very moment—decisions made when the
lure of an exciting career in music dangled in front of me. I
pondered the day I auditioned for entrance to the master's degree program at the Juilliard School of Music in New York
City. I felt the Lord's Spirit bless my performance, and when I
received the news that I had been accepted to study with a renowned teacher and concert pianist, I knew the Lord was
guiding my path. I had set a goal early in life to study music at
Juilliard, to obtain a master's degree, and to bless the lives of

others with the talents the Lord had given me. Those two
years of intensive study and performance were the fulfillment
of a lifelong dream.

But there were other dreams in my life as well, nurtured
from early childhood. As I approached completion of my degree, I spent many hours in prayer to my Father in heaven,
seeking His guidance once again in a major decision. Should I
continue in New York City where I had had so many choice
opportunities and with the promise of many more ahead, or
was there something greater in store? Again prayer, fasting,
and the pondering of my patriarchal blessing brought the answer. I decided to return to Utah upon completion of my degree. I will never forget the expression of shock and disbelief
on the face of my piano teacher in New York as I told her my
decision. It was a decision I have never regretted, for shortly
after I returned, I met a young man who met every criteria
and then some of the person I had always wanted to marry.
This was the Lord's answer. What great joy and happiness
Greg and I have shared in our marriage!

Nothing in my life, not even a concert career, can surpass
in importance the divine calling of being a mother. I have
learned that none of the honors, awards, trophies, and crowns
in the world can compare to the rewards of motherhood. This
is not to say I have given up music to rear a family—far from it.
Music is a very important part of my life and the lives of my
family; it has richly blessed our home and the lives of others.

We are striving in our home to surround our children with
beautiful music ranging from the classic composers to the rich
heritage of Mormon hymns. What a thrill it was recently in
family home evening to hear our 2½-year-old son sing the
first verse of "The Spirit of God Like a Fire Is Burning." Not
all the words were correct, but he sang it with the spirit and
fervor that he had heard so many times on a Mormon Youth
Symphony and Chorus record as well as in our family home
evenings and in sacrament meetings. How exciting it is to see
our children choose the sacred hymns of the Church over
songs heard on radio and television. As I watch our children
gain appreciation for Beethoven and the other great masters,

I'm convinced that it's not that they're musical geniuses, but simply that they are developing a love for this beautiful music through constant exposure. It is true that the more we become acquainted with good music, the more we can learn to enjoy and appreciate it. No one is too old or too young to learn to enjoy good music. Even a young babe loves the hum of a beautiful lullaby.

We have discovered that listening to classical music during mealtimes adds a special spirit to our home. The children take their naps to the inspiring sounds of the Mormon Tabernacle Choir or the Mormon Youth Symphony and Chorus records. At night mommy and daddy sing the children's favorite Primary songs during "cuddle time." What a special time to teach our children the gospel through music! We can plant the tiny seed of testimony, the seed of love for our Heavenly Father and our fellowmen. We've found that our children delight in this and are responding positively to our efforts to instill a love and appreciation for that which is good and uplifting.

When we encourage our children to be music minded, we are making an investment that will yield dividends for a lifetime. Psychologists and musical educators have proven that the study of music has a beneficial influence in the training of the mind. Children who enjoy music usually rank higher scholastically and develop more active imaginations and greater qualities of leadership than do those in homes where love of good music isn't stressed. The slow child, as well as the gifted, can benefit from musical training.

Music improves coordination between thought and action, encourages creative and orderly thinking, fosters mental alertness, and, most important, builds up what we call staying power. Music is often the first artistic activity that makes a child realize that he must work hard to accomplish what he wants.

A musically trained child is conditioned toward split-second accuracy. He learns self-control, and his senses of sight, hearing, and touch are each developed to a high degree. Musical training develops concentration and memory, qualities that will be much needed in his later life and career. Just think what an outstanding gospel scholar a person could be if he were to develop his powers of concentration, allowing him to enlarge his mind more fully through intense scripture study. Musical study helps us to learn this self-mastery and concentration.

Good music is a noble and inspiring gift from God. Through music the Lord inspired many of the greatest men of all times. Leonardo da Vinci listened to the melody of the flute while he painted his masterpiece, the *Mona Lisa*. Albert Einstein, who was known for his genius and his famous theory of relativity, was an accomplished violinist. It is not surprising that music played an important part in the lives of Thomas Jefferson, George Washington, and Albert Schweitzer, who was one of the world's finest exponents of Johann Sebastian Bach.

Arithmetic and abstract concepts are better understood by the musically trained child. In this scientific age, parents can encourage the young scientific mind with music study. A youngster who is trained to understand the complexities of rhythm and the exact relationship of harmonics is more thoroughly prepared to absorb the abstract principles of physics and mathematics. Music, which has been called "mathematics in motion," is a favorite recreation among scientists.

Music is as vital a part of education as the three Rs. The ancient Greeks knew this; they were so aware of the powerful effects of music and of its value in the education of their youth that they gave it an important place in the school curriculum. Modern educators are realizing that music plays a significant role in the lives of today's schoolchildren.

Music can provide deep satisfaction—certain compositions exhilarate and excite; others soothe mind and body. This may be seen in the reactions of a child on hearing the stirring melodies of a military march or the softer tones of a lullaby or gentle hymn. Music is not only a natural stimulus—it is a natural outlet. Creative musical experience provides an effective means of gaining release from tension. This has been true in our home. During cold winter days our little children, filled with the energy children typically have, enjoy playing rhythm instruments, such as the toy drum, rhythm sticks, and song bells. They dance as I play favorite songs for them at the piano. This is a wonderful energy release for them. Often they dance until their rosy cheeks indicate to me a quieter activity is needed.

Some parents regard musical ability as a special gift and think that none but the talented should study. Not so long ago, a child's musical training was abandoned if he did not show signs of genius at seven. Wiser parents realize that finding out where a child's talent lies can be achieved only by consistent study. It is sad to think how many great talents have never been developed simply because the people never knew they had them. The French composer Claude Debussy showed little promise as a child; he lacked even the beginner's enthusiasm at the start of his training. Neither of his parents was musical, and it was not until a former pupil of Chopin heard the boy's half-hearted playing that any real effort was made to encourage him. For a long time, Debussy found difficulty in mastering certain techniques of music, and his teachers were not impressed by his endeavors. But when he became interested, he developed into a serious and dedicated student, and his perseverance prevailed. Today he is recognized as the foremost pioneer in musical impressionism.

I believe that parents are the key influence in their children's attitudes toward music. It lies within their power to make music an investment their children will enjoy throughout their lives, providing beauty, variety, discipline, inspiration, and comfort.

A mother doesn't have to be a music major to teach her children to love good music. She doesn't have to be a trained singer in order for her children to appreciate the hymns of the Church. If she feels musically inadequate, she could simply turn on a record of hymns and sing along with her children. I would encourage families to sing together—to sing in family home evenings and to sing when someone is in a bad mood. Differences in mood and attitude are set aside as everyone sings together. The spirit of the home can quickly be set on the right course. May I paraphrase a famous quotation by saying,

"A family that sings together stays together." Music has a unifying effect. A child will long remember the hours spent singing with parents, brothers, and sisters in the warmth of the family circle.

I have a personal testimony of the power of music to teach, to edify, to bring the human spirit in harmony with the Lord. I also have a testimony of the powerful tool music is in the hands of the adversary. I was appalled as I recently glanced at the list of today's Top Ten popular hits young people listen to. Some of the song titles would be inappropriate to repeat. This music is harmful. It can cause unworthy thoughts that can lead to unworthy actions. I would pray that parents would keep these evil influences from coming into their homes and teach their children to shun them.

Motherhood is a sacred responsibility and blessing. Mothers can expose their children to the beauties of life and instill in them a love for that which uplifts and edifies. One of the basic beliefs of The Church of Jesus Christ of Latter-day Saints is found in the thirteenth Article of Faith: "If there is anything virtuous, lovely, or of good report or praiseworthy, we seek after these things." It is sad that in our society today, we are bombarded with so much that debases and corrupts human lives.

Judicious mothers realize that they hold a powerful position for good. Strengthening the family is more vital with each passing day, as new challenges to the strength and solidarity of the home arise. Never before in history have so many insidious influences threatened the family. Many of these influences come right into the home, often uninvited, over the radio and television airwaves and in newspapers, magazines, books, and other literature. Mothers are in a frontline position to guard against these degrading influences. A wise mother will actively guard against movies, radio and television programs, and music that could corrupt the lives of her children. She will teach her children to seek good reading material and see that only good reading material enters the home. She will help her children develop a love for good music rather than for music with suggestive lyrics and style. Unrestrained exposure to these unsavory influences sows the seeds for tearing down family life. It is well known that the early years are the most important in forming a child's character and abilities. A mother's love and example are critically important at this time in her children's lives.

As the mother of four small children, I am constantly aware of the tremendous responsibility I have to teach my children true principles that will enable them to travel life's highways with confidence and will give them faith to brave life's storms. Successful family life takes more diligent effort and skill than any other endeavor in life, for we are not merely working with statistics, computers, legal matters, or inventories; rather, we are shaping and molding divine lives to become productive, independent, and, most of all, happy human beings.

With the Lord Jesus Christ as our source of power, we can provide our homes with stability and direction, and, as we do so, we can surround our children with the beauty and happiness that abound in life and that eternity can hold in store for them.

Sally Peterson Brinton has a bachelor's degree from the University of Utah and a master's degree from the Juilliard School of Music. A concert pianist, she was first-place winner of two national piano competitions and has performed as guest soloist with orchestras throughout the United States. She made her New York debut at Lincoln Center in 1975. As Miss Utah 1972, she participated in the Miss America Pageant and was winner of the Miss Congeniality and talent awards. In the Church she has been a stake Young Women president, stake music chairman, and counselor in Relief Society and Primary presidencies. She and her husband, Dr. Gregory S. Brinton, have four children. They have been residing in Brookfield, Wisconsin, and plan to make their home in Salt Lake City.

A Musical Stewardship— Teacher of Life

JoAnn Ottley

As a confirmed people watcher, I have come to believe that a sense of humor is perhaps one of the highest of man's attributes. That, of course, gives rise to the question of whether our Heavenly Father has a sense of humor, and if so, how it could possibly be manifest. However, watching many lives over the years, our own included, leads me to believe that a Divine sense of humor, which I definitely do believe exists, may most often be exhibited in the form of surprises, one of which is finding myself occupying a position as lecturer—a long way from being a musician. I am constantly amazed at the variety of opportunities and assignments that come my way because I am a music maker, more specifically because I am a music maker in the name of the Lord.

Much reflection has gone into preparation for this assignment, especially about the years that prepared my husband and me for the situation in which we now find ourselves. I've thought about the little girl who simply loved music and preferred practicing over most everything—certainly above helping with the dishes; about the young boy who gave his all to the trombone, even when his body was so small he had to reach the farthest position of the slide with his foot.

My husband and I frequently still look at each other in various situations and say, "What in the world are we doing here?" There is a difference when one aspires to certain things and plans his life in a certain way, but when the Lord deals in surprises, as He does, within the confines of the Kingdom, His children often find themselves doing some large-scale adapting.

Aspiring young singers looking toward musical careers sometimes ask us for some advice. The advice my husband and I most frequently give is the advice given by a famous musician who was asked by a young aspirant whether he should pursue a career in music. The musician said, "If anything can keep you out of music, let it." Only those who are musicians know what that means. It is simply that the life of a performing musician should be pursued only by those willing to pay an enormous price. Let's look at some of the price tags.

A large percentage of the time, performers feel as if they are walking down the mouth of a hungry lion, or that they are nude under a microscope. Forgive me if that sounds a little crude, but as a performer stands before an audience, especially a recital audience, she seems totally exposed—every sound, every breath, every thought, every feeling. There are, as a matter of fact, many dropouts in the world of singing simply because of terror. There are many with great talent who simply cannot handle the fire.

One might be surprised, actually, at some of the big names in the performing business who are still terrified. A great opera star a generation back threw up in a bucket offstage before every performance. That is terror. Just a couple of years ago, the Tabernacle Choir performed a concert with John Denver. We might expect John Denver to be the most all-together, cool, confident person imaginable, and my husband was feeling a little bit nonplussed about working with him, but John Denver was shaking in his boots! The trick for the performer, of course, lies in concealing the terror and performing well regardless.

There are other terrors. Several years ago, for instance, in the middle of a very difficult solo on the Tabernacle Choir broadcast, I suddenly found myself all alone without accompaniment and no inkling whether or when it might return. My internal dialogue with myself went something like this: "Now what are my choices? I can stop singing, I can let the terror engulf me and allow the TV cameras to see just how I feel, or I can continue singing and hope that at some point the organist will join me. I might end up doing an unaccompanied solo— and this is definitely not the right piece for it." I just kept singing. As I came to the crucial moment when the voice part ends and the accompaniment takes over, there was Brother Robert J. Cundick with the organ. He had had his own crisis at the keyboard—a stuck key. We survived, older and wiser.

And one night at a very important concert, I went offstage between groups of songs to take a drink of water and poured the whole thing down the front of my gown. What could I do? There was no choice but to go back on. I tried to hold my hands gracefully to cover up the long dark streak, and if anyone noticed, at least they were kind enough not to tell me. May I add that there was a bonus attendant to this crisis: the shock was so unnerving that it pulverized all my stage fright, serving to give me a startlingly dynamic performance of the aria that followed.

No wonder there are a lot of dropouts!

Perhaps the greatest risk in the music business is its tendency to consume the individual. It could so easily devour all one's devotion—mind, body, and spirit—and time. At our house we have a constant intense battle (not between us but together) to preserve our family's identity and private pursuits removed from the musical world and from the Tabernacle Choir. Not too long after my husband was called to the position of Tabernacle Choir conductor, while he was just learning to handle this big business into which he had been plunged, with all the publicity and all the attention and all the pressure and all the changes, our teenage son said, "I think I like the old Dad better—not Saint Jerold!" I should clarify that he was not talking about his father's demeanor at home, but only the public attention he was getting.

Recently (and this one is not so amusing—it hurt a little) we received a letter from some friends who were temple missionaries in New Zealand. These are very dear friends, the kind who scold us when we need it, as we do for them, and in the letter they carefully and tactfully said they had heard from friends that Jerry and I were both so busy that we were virtually living separate lives. Now, that is a great misunderstanding. It is not true, but it points out another danger of this business: that virtually everything we do is in the papers, and it *appears* we are gone and performing every minute of the day and night. They don't know I am still home vacuuming. They don't know I'm home to chat with my daughter as she arrives from school every day. They don't know how hard I am struggling to fulfill all the areas of my individual stewardship.

Vulnerability is another trademark of the singer. William Walker, a famous baritone, said, "The singer is the most vulnerable of all artists. He takes his heart out of his body, extends it to the audience and says, 'Love me.'" And may I add, "Allow me to love you." Many people can't handle the immense exposure of the heart that is entailed in singing.

There is more to the issue of vulnerability. There are those two tiny bands of tissue called vocal cords. They are sensitive, they are fragile, and everything rests on them. A little draft, a bit of nausea, a sleepless night, a quarrel or a disappointment, or just a little sunburn, and they are affected. I have thought, for instance, about a violinist preparing for a performance, opening his case, and finding, as he pulls his instrument from the case, that it has suddenly turned to rubber. That's similar to what a singer faces, because the slightest little thing can alter the instrument. It is no wonder that singers are renowned for being strange, for there are ample reasons for it. It's a bit like living on a tight wire strung over a long, deep ravine—very exciting and very perilous.

It is interesting to compare singing to athletics. I don't know much about the disadvantages athletes face, but I think they have some advantages. For instance, a stopwatch or measuring tape tells very simply how well they have performed. There is no question. Music, however, occupies time rather than space, and when it's done, it's gone. There is no way to know whether we have succeeded except from the reactions of the people for whom we have sung. People often pay me some lovely compliment and add, ". . . but I'm sure you have already heard that a thousand times. You don't need to hear it from me." "On the contrary," I often say, "that is the only way I know whether I did what I came here to do."

Athletes are allowed errors—not encouraged, but allowed. In some cases the errors are even tallied up on the scoreboard. Singers don't have that privilege. What happens if I crack about three times on my high notes in performances? That's it. No more JoAnn as a soprano. I may be able to change and become something that doesn't require high notes, but just a few bad crucial tones and my life is changed.

I love to watch athletic contests and see the grimacing and perspiration on the faces of the athletes. Do you know that singers work just about that hard? Do you know how hard we're working inside, under that glossy facade? Do you realize that it's like heavy athletics? Whether we are in fancy gowns or forty-pound opera costumes, often we work just as hard as the athlete. As listeners, however, you have no idea. If you do know how hard we're working, we have partly failed, because you are not supposed to be able to see that in our art. Heaven forbid any visible perspiration! Handel's *Messiah,* for instance, presents a rather different kind of physical challenge for the soprano, who must sit very still on stage, in view of the entire audience, for some forty-five minutes before she sings one note. By the time the moment arrives for her to sing, a delicate, exposed entrance, she feels that all her blood is pooled somewhere in the vicinity of her big toe, and she wonders whether there is even a tone in her. My hidden fantasy for many years has been the opportunity of just once waiting until the moment to begin singing and then bounding onto the stage, all warmed up, in a sweat suit.

Now, with such problems, you may ask, why are there fifty

singers for every one opportunity in the singing business? Why are thousands of people constantly preparing for vocal careers in spite of all these detractions? I'd like to share some things I am gleaning from my life as a singer that will perhaps answer these questions.

One great benefit would have to be self-discovery. Singing has perhaps done nothing greater for me than helping me discover hidden parts of myself. I fully believe there are no boring people in this life, but only unexplored, unexcavated places in souls. And I have watched, as a singing teacher, even the youngest, most timid beginners begin to unfold and blossom as they begin to sing. For a singer this continues on through ever-increasing challenges, each of which teaches more about oneself and about life in general.

Next might be the discovery of my body as an instrument. For singers, the body *is* the instrument. Sometimes it is really not willing to do what we ask of it. Some days we have to get very sly to get it to obey us. It just sits there and dares us to get anything out of it. Eventually we learn what we need to do in order to get the job done regardless. The body has astonishing capacities, and the act of singing involves an all-encompassing use of the body—not merely the vocal cords, but muscle systems throughout the body. The breathing mechanism is large and complex and difficult. Good posture is vital. If a singer doesn't carry her body perfectly, she can't sing well. A singer must learn a lot about the body and mastery of it.

Several years ago I was invited to do my first *Carmina Burana* with Ballet West. That production involves not only dancers, but also a full symphony, a choir, and three soloists. It was an amazing experience, as those of us in the combined artistic forces watched each other work for the first time. The dancers couldn't believe what the singers could do, and the singers couldn't believe what the dancers could do. One of the dancers asked me if I sang with my breath going both in and out. (I wish I could—just think of the phrases I could sing!) She honestly wondered, and I felt the same about the things the dancers were doing. I thought surely they must be doing it with mirrors, because no body should be capable of doing what those bodies were doing. We had a great time of mutual admiration as we saw the great heights and depths to which talents can be brought.

I have learned a lot about the laws of health. It is absolutely necessary to stay well. Singers frequently find, for instance, that with constant use, the throat becomes very susceptible to every passing problem. I would swear that if I get a hangnail, it affects my throat. Everything goes to the throat, and in order to perform well, it is necessary for a singer to learn much about how to stay healthy.

Opera singing in particular is a big teacher—a cruel schoolmaster, in a way. It may be that there is not on the earth anything that makes a more nearly complete demand on a human than opera. First, it takes all of the mind. There have been times when I expected smoke to begin trickling out through my ears as I put my poor brain on overload trying to get a full score registered in there. In each of the operas I have done in the last few years, there have been between 100 and 150 pages to learn—not only my own part, but that of anyone else who is on stage at the same time—and in a foreign language. It is necessary to know what each person is saying, all of the implications, and all of the words. It is necessary to know hundreds—thousands—of notes and exactly when to sing them and where to take each breath. It is vital to know the orchestral part as well, not only as accompaniment but also to be able to get immediately back on track in case of error.

Opera demands the total body. Singing ranks with heavy labor or athletics in terms of energy output. Add to that heavy (often twenty to forty pounds), cumbersome costumes. Even dying on stage requires far more energy than I ever dreamed.

And the emotions. Opera, I have come to believe, is largely about human feeling. The plots are often sick, but I suspect they are largely excuses for exhibiting, with great music, not only the voice but also human emotion at its extremes. Opera requires the total package of humanity all at once, and it is a glorious feeling to know that our total being has been challenged to its fullest and has survived—occasionally even conquered.

Life as a singer has taught me some things about risks. We Mormons are a conservative lot—sometimes, I fear, un-explored. I think we need to be just a bit bolder, not *in spite* of commandments but *because* of them. I think we need to risk failing a little more. We singers take the risks of not being liked, and we take many risks inherent in the music. As performers we hear the term "break a leg." That used to bother me until I finally figured out what it meant. It means go out and give it everything, including the risk of breaking a leg, figuratively speaking. Be willing to deliver all we can find in ourselves and in the music.

Musical stewardship provides one of its nicest functions as it exercises us in beauty. I have been making music since I was nine years old, and I began singing lessons at the age of fifteen. I know that some music has the power to degrade and pull down, but I am keenly aware of the beauty that has passed through my soul. The music itself and the words—the most noble, the most passionate, the most divinely worshipful words of the greatest poets in five or six languages—all that beauty has passed through me and has had an effect. How grateful I am to have been a conduit for that beauty, passing it on to others. It is a joyous way to fulfill the Savior's admonition to feed His sheep.

I have not always been convinced of the value of singing. I didn't used to think it was very important, but one day a lady said to me after a Relief Society program, tears streaming down her face, "Sister Ottley, how you enrich our lives." And one night a sister came up to me after I had sung in a sacrament meeting and said, "Thank you, JoAnn. Tonight I needed to be sung to." Comments such as these go a long way to show me the value of singing in a troubled world.

Singing can provide a valuable school in gospel principles and in their understanding and application. This is the best area of all, and sometimes it is overlooked. Take the subject of humility, for instance. This was one of the subjects about which I had to learn some big lessons very early. Imagine what kind of performance a singer would give if she were to stand backstage and say, "Oh, I'm not much of a singer. I can't really

do this job very well. Someone else could do it much better."
She wouldn't get many further invitations. I had to find out
quickly what humility truly is. I knew that, since I had been
commanded to be humble, I'd better figure it out. Do you
know what it is? Yes, it is teachableness, but it is more. It is, as
one author wrote, "a right estimate of ourselves as God sees
us." It is a correct estimate. It is giving credit where the credit
is due, to the Lord and to others, and passing the honors upward to Him.

I have learned reliance on the Lord. I think sometimes He
must get weary of my asking for miracles, but oh, how many
times I have faced moments when there was a big performance to do and no voice! I am prone to bronchitis, and many
times with a crucial performance to do and a critically im-
paired voice, I have had a priesthood blessing, have spent
much time on my knees, and have somehow had the voice appear just long enough to do the singing, sometimes including
the highest, softest notes, then had the voice disappear immediately after the performance, not to be usable again for
weeks. I've had many opportunities for seeking and submit-
ting to the Lord's will.

It is easy to get so caught up in pursuing professional
things that we forget the big picture. We need to remember
our promises to the Lord and let Him call the shots. The decisions are often painful, and there is a constant wrestling with
priorities and balances, but we have learned profoundly at our
house that the Lord's ideas for us as individuals, as His children, are much greater than our own. We Latter-day Saints
have been accused, and sometimes rightly so, of being mind-
less lemmings. That shot has been fired at us many times because we seek to do "the Lord's will." But those people don't
know what we know—that if somehow we can align ourselves
so as to discern His design for us and follow it, we end up
much greater, much higher, much happier than if we follow
our own self-made design.

"Be ye therefore perfect"—not as a conductor, not as a
singer, not as a ball player, but as an entire person. I re-

member President J. Reuben Clark saying years ago that he didn't think anybody was going to be able to fancy-dribble a ball past St. Peter. Nor is JoAnn going to be able to sing a big, flashy aria and get to the celestial kingdom. I like the term used by Elder Neal A. Maxwell, "symmetrical development." May I relate a story about that subject.

Several years ago I was invited to sing with an orchestra under a very famous up-and-coming young conductor. The choir had repeated one particular spot in the score several times, and he was not getting what he wanted from them. At that moment the conductor of the choir, who had prepared them for the concert, walked over to the conductor and quietly suggested the need for a cue from the conductor at the point where the difficulty was occurring. The conductor went into an absolute rage. He stamped up and down on the podium, grabbed his towel, left the podium, and went to his room. The choir leader, a personal friend of ours, came over to me and said, "JoAnn, did you ever see anything like that?" I replied, "Yes, I spank my three-year-old for it."

That was one of many learning moments for me in my people-watching. Many persons in the performing business haven't learned about "symmetrical development." They have learned to be giants in the musical world, but they are still midgets in other areas of their lives. It is not enough to grow in one area only. We will take the entire package back to our Father in heaven. (I must add here that I have also become acquainted with many in the music business who have developed seemingly every facet of their beings to giant proportions.)

Not long ago I read a biography of one of the greatest divas of all time, and as I came to the end of that book I thought my heart would break. Perhaps never have I felt more compassion for an individual, because regardless of great fame and fortune, she lived her entire life without joy. I have more joy in an hour than she had in a lifetime.

Man is that he might have joy. I believe music exists for the purpose of joy in a tough world, healing, blessing, and lifting lives. By and large I think it succeeds. Its power to bring joy, however, encompasses both its greatest gift and its greatest danger. Its power is so great, in fact, that we can easily be swayed to make it an object rather than a tool of worship.

As a singer I have had many sublime moments—moments when I have felt bathed in light and a profound sense of oneness with my Maker. These are inexpressibly choice times. I suspect that it is the overwhelming yearning for such moments of companionship with truth and light and spirit that entices drug-users to what they interpret as joy even though it destroys their bodies and enslaves their souls. Music has some of those same powers. It is rewarding and joyous and consuming to the point where it can addict and devour our lives, both as performers and as consumers.

A musician friend in New York City said to me recently, "I am coming to resent the love I have for what I do." His career is going badly, and I believe the problem, unknown to him, is that his joy is based on music and his life as a musician. If my musical involvement ended tomorrow, I would probably shed some tears and it would be painful, but my overall joy would remain intact because I know something this friend doesn't know, something the great diva died without knowing. I know that while music is a great joy, it is only a delicious fragment of a greater joy, even a promised fullness of joy.

I am grateful to be a music maker. I am grateful for the effect that music has had on my life and for whatever joy I have been able to bring to others. Beyond that, however, is the gratitude that I know precisely what this gift is: a gift from God. It is not the whole forest; it is only one shining tree.

I yearn to sing in the language of Adam, pure and undefiled. I hope I can learn it. I want to meet the great composers—Brahms and Beethoven and Mozart and the others—and I want to ask them, "Did I come anywhere near what you had in mind when you composed that magnificent music?" I think I sang before I came here, and I think I'll sing after I leave, but it doesn't matter. All mankind yearns for the joy I have within me, and my greatest gratitude is for this joy, born not of music but of God and His Son and the fullness of the gospel.

God is in His heaven; He loves us, and His greatest gifts are ours. All we have to do is love Him. May I leave you with a statement from President Spencer W. Kimball: "Let us get our instruments tightly strung and our melodies sweetly sung. Let us not die with our music still in us. Let us rather use this precious mortal probation to move confidently and gloriously upward toward the eternal life which God our Father gives to those who keep His commandments." (From a program honoring President Kimball on his eightieth birthday. March 28, 1975.)

JoAnn Ottley has performed in concert, opera, and recital throughout the United States and Europe. She has been soloist with major symphony orchestras and choruses, with Ballet West, and with the Mormon Tabernacle Choir, and has sung leading roles with Utah Opera Company. She is currently vocal coach for the Tabernacle Choir. She and her husband, Tabernacle Choir conductor Jerold Ottley, also share an assignment as gospel doctrine teachers. Sister Ottley studied at the University of Utah and Brigham Young University, and was a Fulbright Scholar in Cologne, West Germany, where she was a pupil of Josef Metternich at Staatliche Hochschule für Musik. In the Church she has taught in youth and adult classes and has been president, dance director and speech director for the Young Women's organization, as well as served in music capacities. She and Brother Ottley have two children.

The Bread and Milk of Living

Eileen Gibbons Kump

We have a Father in heaven who loves us. The gospel of
Jesus Christ—and not some other—is true. Because the Holy
Ghost is with us, we are blessed with light, comfort, and
stamina. The kind, far-seeing purposes of God in giving us
such a life—and even chastisements along the way—bring us
gradually to know that we are dependent upon powers far
greater than our own. The fact that sooner or later we must
come to realize that dependence presents a paradox to me as a
woman.

Here we are, working through our daily lives, often into
the wind, discovering who we are and what is important not
just eternally but before lunch! We fill many roles and search
for serenity as life rises and falls between the blessings of
heaven and a bedrock of testimony and faith. Daily as women
we strive for all we are worth to use our resources to the ut-
most, to give form and relevance to our many activities, to do
nothing unimportant, and to enjoy it all.

I am convinced that as we gradually come to understand

our dependence upon our Father in heaven, we also come to know our need to depend upon ourselves and to bring forth the best that we possess in order to live this tough life with style, with bouyancy, meaningfully, using our heads.

Writing is one of the ways through which I reach for order in my life, for enjoyment, and for the best that is in me. Since my marriage, deciding whether to write at all has been a hard decision because there are so many responsibilities and so many options. Why do it then?

Even in a room occupied by others, writing time is time alone with myself. It carries a feeling of independence, a private freedom, and even success now and then, because enduring to the end of a short story is so much shorter than the other kind. When I am writing a story, all requirements are self-imposed. They come from the inside out instead of *at* me. No one waits. Thus the usual direction of my anxieties is reversed and relaxed. A right word can be found when I find it, and the story finished whenever it is done.

This is not to say that writing is easy. It is rigorous. Everything in the anticipated story must fit it. The word search is meticulous, often long and discouraging, sometimes abandoned. There is always in the struggle the feeling that a perfect story lies buried beneath layers of nonsense super-glued together to make the excavation difficult. That the excavation is never completely successful doesn't matter because the search is exhilarating. It requires focus, concentration, and fine tools. The walls of the mind must be made to soften and to move. Every line must be shaped to the whole, made true to the eye and the ear and the heart. Dialogue must be authentic and purposeful without seeming to be purposeful at all. Flashes of genius must be scratched and a line born of a week's labor refined out of existence. Emotion and idea must rise from the page like a mist that cannot be seen or anticipated and is therefore always felt with astonishment.

My justification for stealing what time I can for writing lies in these experiences: the freedom, the occasional success, the difficulty. But the choice is never simple because the telephone rings, appointments must be made and kept, hands

and voices interrupt—and there is the laundry. Procrastina-
tion eventually becomes impossible because there are no clean
socks. Hunger asserts itself, destroying good natures, and my
house is not yet self-cleaning. Church service must still be
given by the individual.

But I do have time to think—and one of the things I think
about most is the bread and milk of living, or, in other words,
how to make daily life my friend. Mortality should be an adventure, not a burden.

Many years ago when our son was six, he made his first basket. It had been a long pursuit. He can still feel the heaviness
of that basketball and remember how high the hoop seemed to
be.

When he made the basket, he came running into the house
to tell me about it. Sharing his excitement, I said, "Hurry back
outside and see if you can make another one!"

"No," he said. "First I have to draw a picture of me making
it."

That moment—unforgettable, puzzling—slowed me down.
It made me thoughtful. It captured the intensity of human experience and forced me to confront myself.

All of us make our first basket, but do we stop and draw a
picture of us making it? In other words, do we think about
what we do? Do we pause from doing to reflect? Do we assign
importance to the small daily happenings of our lives by giving
them our attention? Do we preserve them somehow?

Or do we fly past them with the velocity of a Honda, slow-
ing down when the major disruptions of life occur but otherwise mostly speed-reading the repetition and deceptive trivia
that occupy so much of our time?

In my short story titled "God Willing," Grandma Amy has
just had a heart spell and has decided that she had better
finally get around to writing down a few words for her pos-

terity. At that moment, grandchildren bickering over the porch swing holler for her to come and referee:

"The yell faded but Amy was already on her feet and out the front door as if she were well to make Jess either share or go weed half a row of onions. . . . Jess moved over of course but Amy went back inside trembling and melancholy. Why had she grabbed the swing, and even shaken the pencil in Jess' face? Was that necessary? How were they to become acquainted with their old friend mortality if she kept smoothing things out for them? She must think, darn it! She mustn't make life too soft." (Eileen G. Kump, *Bread and Milk and Other Stories*, Provo: BYU Press, 1979, p. 85.)

Grandma Amy needn't worry about whether her posterity will make the acquaintance of her old friend mortality. They will, even if she meddles. The question is, will they become its friends or remain simply acquaintances? All of us meet mortality. Not all of us befriend her. How is that done? By drawing pictures of our baskets? Yes.

As I was growing up, I was held by my grandmother's stories about her childhood. Finally, about thirty years ago I began a five-year interrogation during which I would ask questions and she would write her memories, one by one. I persisted, seeking more detail, sending her in dusty directions.

Both of us were amazed at what happened. Her mind flew, lighted, flew once more. Her heart felt again and again the original pain and pleasure of all her years. Back and forth from one end of Utah to the other went our letters—or one of us—until finally we realized that we had better organize what she had written into chapters and type it up. I hurried to do this because both of us could see that what we had loosed could not be contained. In fact, her memory muscles had so relaxed by this time that she continued to send experiences for the rest of her life. There are two supplements to her life story.

There had been much more to write about than she thought there was when she began remembering. And something even more unexpected happened. When she contemplated the finished product, held it and read it and laughed and cried, she was astounded at the richness of her life. She could not remember doing much noticing, let alone thinking about what had happened to her, as she went along. Yet now that she could stand back and look at the whole of it and relive it and see herself written and shared with others, she was pleased with mortality. It hadn't let her down after all.

Another experience not too long afterward brought me down a different road to a similar wisdom. Enrollment in graduate school in California required only my second trip away from Utah. In our writing workshop were people from all backgrounds. I was not embarrassed to be from Utah or for being a Mormon, but I felt apologetic for my scant experience and for the only subject I had written fiction about in the past—my family. I had been writing what I thought were clever little narratives about the crazy things our family had done to keep up financially, but the sophistication and intellect of my new surroundings pulled me away, and I turned to more sensational subjects for my short stories.

Finally I said to our director, "I don't have anything to write about."

Impatient, almost angry, he said, "Yes you do. You just don't know it. There isn't a person in that workshop who wouldn't gladly trade his experience for yours."

I knew that he was referring to Mormon history and culture, but he was also encouraging me to value my *own* experience.

After that, I quit manufacturing brittle pieces about racial prejudice and thwarted romance, about which I knew nothing. I looked again at my own life, at what I knew best, and considered again my grandmother and the richness that had excited her when she wrote her life story.

Grandmother's life had first attracted me as a writer because of the historical significance of her childhood in the United Order. That needed to be recorded. But aside from such historical significance, she really had not done much or been much on the scales by which we weigh importance. She had buried one of her ten babies. She had seen her husband off on a mission when she was expecting their fourth child. Later she lost him to cancer. There were always money worries and her rheumatism.

I began to see that the beauty and disappointments of her life, the pulse of it, the heartbeat, yes the richness and the power, lay in the little everyday happenings that formed its greatest part: soapmaking day; gathering sand with which to scour the knives, forks, and spoons; the square of cheese that sometimes lay beside the nightly meal of bread and milk; the cape a beau slipped through the window on Christmas Eve; the despised schoolteacher, and the adored one; the best dress—the only Sunday one—ruined at the grist mill (Could it ever be replaced? When?); the pain of being scolded by a young husband for putting too much salt on his boiled egg; his long legs at family prayer time when it was so hard to find kneeling space in the small kitchen.

Such experiences were the essence of her life; that's why I used them in my fiction. There is importance, even magic, in the mundane, in the bread and milk of living. It is one way to arrive at truth. It is a sure way to befriend mortality and make life an adventure.

Willa Cather spoke of her childhood home, Nebraska, as a storehouse of literary material. I have crossed Nebraska at least twenty times. The landscape is only slightly more exciting than Wyoming's. (I do like both—because I have a home at each end.) But Willa Cather saw richness there, an inexhaustible supply of material for her stories. "Everywhere," she said, "is a storehouse of literary material." Everywhere. "The only need is the eye to see." (Mildred Bennett, *The World of Willa Cather,* Lincoln: University of Nebraska Press, 1961, p. 93.) She chose to write about the small undulations on life's landscape, realizing, I'm sure, that imagination is not the capacity to invent what is not there, but the capacity to see and use what is there. How important it is that we have the imagination to value our experience.

Latter-day Saints view mortality with affection. If we are writers, or selective readers, we know that a poem or short story has the power to give form and relevance to our lives.

The writer looks at the sequence of common days, sculpts out a scene or emotion or act or even a color or texture, and thinks on it until she feels it and owns it and can shape it with language into a poem or story with a beginning and an end. Then she gives it back to us so that we can have an experience we slighted the first time around or perhaps missed altogether.

My decision to dwell on everyday happenings in my stories has been deliberate. There is drama there. Shaping can give it relevance. Besides, sometimes we become caught up in the lie that there is such a thing as an uneventful day. I want to write stories that reveal how extraordinary the ordinary can be when we don't speed-read it.

A good story or poem illuminates human behavior in some way, throwing light into the shade, exposing unlikely moments to the power of language. The gospel gives us our greatest insight into the nature and meaning of existence, but literature can help. Through it also we have great experience; we nod at the truth about mortality that emerges from these experiences. In good art as in true religion, what we know is verified. We come to understand ourselves and others better. Whether it is about death or simply dishwashing, a boil or a simple blister, a poem or story helps me become objective about myself. It enables me to put a little distance between me and life. And since it is impossible to read life with my forehead resting on the page, literature helps me to stand back far enough to see.

Willa Cather insisted that "artistic appreciation should include all the activities of life." She wrote: "The farmer's wife who raises a large family and cooks for them and makes their clothes and keeps house and on the side runs a truck garden and a chicken farm and a canning establishment, and . . . enjoys doing it all, and doing it well, contributes more to art than all the culture clubs." (Bennett, *op. cit.*, p. 167.)

I knew such an artist. My father-in-law always planted his sugar beets in April or May and then within two or three days, much too early, he was out kneeling in the dirt, scratching and searching for the first sign of green life. He knew the sugar beets would grow. But his love of the farm and his excitement about that tiny earth-shaking miracle was so great that he had to be there!

Among my friends are four women who are artists. Surely they have a friendship with life. They are all human, with weaknesses and problems. But they are artists.

I am thinking first of a sister in our ward in Missouri whose regard for others gives significance to every encounter. She never just walks on by; in her presence, we like ourselves. Her manner with everyone is not simply warm—it is interested. It is not simply interested—it is encouraging. She never lets you down. Such refinement in human relationships is not simply personality—it is art. Must she paint or write or dance, or even read books, to be a creative woman? Of course not.

Another sister can decide at 11 A.M. to have pie for lunch. I have never seen flour and shortening and intuition maneuvered with such efficiency and style. She begins; it is done. She is timid in public life, afraid to teach a class in church or even pray. But when she is making a pie she is comfortable. She is an artist in an important corner of her life where hesitancy and doubt are nonexistent.

Part of my legacy as a Latter-day Saint woman is another grandmother who buried seven of her twelve children, but who never let go of an ideal. After being married for many months with no child on the way, she said pleadingly to her husband, "Will we never have children?" Through his priesthood, he promised her that they would.

When she was expecting a child, she did her work sitting in a chair. She nurtured and weeded her garden moving along the rows in a small wagon. She spent weeks in bed before and after the birth of each baby.

At the death of a child—whether a few hours old or age twelve, twenty-three, or thirty-three—amid tears, a final kiss on the cheek, and a whispered promise of eventual reunion, she clung to her divine devotion to motherhood. No pain or loss ever shook her from the path her feet had taken, the commitment she had made to bearing children no matter what it cost her.

Was she an artist? Why not? Art is form. Art is meaning.

And her commitment to an idea gave form and relevance to everything she ever did.

Another friend is an expert in husband-treating. Looking at myself, a wife exasperated by a dropped sock or a closet door left open, I am awed by her accomplishment. The governing thought of each day seems to be to please her husband, to help him, to make their home pleasant. When he walks into the kitchen where she is working, the rest of her world seems to fall back into shadow. He is the center. This sister is not demonstrative. I don't even know what she does. Is it her trust? her innate unselfishness? Well, it is wonderful to see. She is an artist.

Another creative activity that breeds optimism and self-knowledge and shapes our lives is journal-keeping. It is talked about so much nowadays that we may make the mistake of not doing it just to be different. But it is a crucial assignment—in my opinion, necessary and beyond value. Why? Because daily recording forces us to confront ourselves daily. We must select and then write happenings before we have time to worry about whether they are important enough to record. Never waste time enjoying such worry. We cannot weigh importance on the scene, and we should not sort what happens to us into bins as if moments were apples or potatoes.

Memory is proof that our emotions are engaged just as honestly and readily by small events as by large. What do we remember? Years? Weeks? Days? I doubt it. Moments? More than likely. And only towering times? No. Trivia? Yes. Anything can be tender to the touch of memory.

Then what do we write in our journals? Almost anything. Nearly everything. We decide, but for goodness' sake we shouldn't worry about whether it is important enough. If it even whispers of feeling or interest, we should write it down. Do that to a happening and we have rescued it forever from being trivial. Think about it as well, and we have quadrupled its value in bringing us and mortality into warm friendship. As we write, we should not summarize our days—summaries have no heartbeat. One event told with detail will radiate our history in all directions.

A young woman who enrolled in a writing class of mine several years ago had married at eighteen. As part of her preparation to leave home, she wrote a detailed story of her life to that time—the proms and the crushes on boys, her friends, the births of her little brothers, everything she could remember. Within about three years of her wedding she lost her father in a violent accident that also left her mother partly paralyzed; she nearly lost a premature baby boy; and she underwent surgery for fast-spreading cancer. Would she ever, now, go back and record the first eighteen years of her life? Wouldn't it seem too frivolous? unimportant? Wouldn't the exuberance and youthful thrills be overshadowed forever? They deserved attention, and because she gave it in time, they are preserved in such a way that her sons and daughters will read them and identify with them and know their mother better.

We live in the present, and when we write it now, we are bringing a perspective impossible later on. A little boy drew a picture of himself making a basket. It is preserved. We should encourage our children to recognize the value of their experiences. Sometimes a teacher will send children off into writing only fantasy or concoction. If children can learn to write about their own lives, however uneventful they may seem to an adult, and if they can then share them with others, they will realize both their universality and their uniqueness. Children's lives need shape and meaning too.

May I share a note from one of our daughters, our only journal-keeper. She was not leaving on a mission or for college. She was in the sixth grade, and she was going to school, as she had to do every single day. And it was tough. "When I'm leaving you, it is hard and I want to cry, but don't you be upset or worry because when I get to school I'll be okay because I'll get busy and I won't think about home any more—until it gets near lunch time."

Is that an earth-shaking experience? Of course. Was her life as formless after she wrote those penetrating thoughts as it was before? No. That simple act of writing gave form and relevance to her daily pain. The note will be precious to her forever. And look how much importance her simple observations took on when she wrote them down!

Art and our journals help us value each moment of each day. They help us relish life as we go. So does simply recognizing the richness of daily life and pacing ourselves to enjoy it. I come to you from a kitchen table in Missouri. It is the concrete center of my life. Seated there I pay the bills, answer the phone, plan supper, keep our family journal, write letters, think, agonize over after-school snacks, and prepare my Sunday School lesson. When there is time—and sometimes when there isn't—I write stories.

From where I sit I can see through the glass of our 1912 front door. At 2:30 P.M., I become fidgety, excited, happier. I cannot keep my eyes from the door. At least ten minutes are wasted, although I know better, and then up the walk come three high school students. My senses are alive. The family is coming home! Books litter the foyer instead of going to their shelves, but I will scold about that later. My Israel is gathering, and as soon as Dad and the other girl arrive, we will all be under one roof.

This happens almost every day, yet it is a highlight of my life. I am overwhelmed with a sense of its importance. Such fleeting moments need our attention and thought. Happiness lies so much in knowing that what is happening may be earth-shaking—not just in being there and moving on.

In our city two elementary schools will be permanently closed this fall. Three hundred twenty-five children (about two hundred families) will be affected. Newspaper headlines, editorials, local talk shows, and hot-tempered board meetings have all reflected the importance of the decision to close these schools.

One afternoon during this city-wide furor, a much quieter event took place. A supervisor of student teachers visited a headstart classroom of four-year-olds. He took a seat at the back where he could observe the teacher trainee. He didn't see the little boy standing in front of him until the child held up his arms and said, "Hold me." The supervisor took the boy on his knee and turned his attention back to the front of the room. The next time he looked down, a line of children stood in front of him waiting for a turn.

Of course event one—the closing of schools—is important. Is it more important? The bread and milk of living is illustrated in the second episode, yet it was registered by only one person, the supervisor. It surely never made the newspapers.

It is the depth of experience that matters, not the breadth. Breadth we measure in newspapers, maps, calendars, mementos, and picture postcards. But depth is silent and invisible, awaiting discovery—or creation. It is a gold mine awaiting the miner's tool. We are the miners.

I have a line or two from a letter of a great-aunt who lived with her family but was isolated from them by old age and illness, seemingly done with real living at eighty-two. Note how she felt about old age: "I am ashamed that I would let a little misery block out the wonderful opportunity to think, to study, and connect my life's experiences with the truths which I was too self-engrossed to see as I went along. But it never occurred to me that a period of time would be given me when there was nothing else to do but *think,* and learn. See how foolish of me to think there was nothing for me to do! There is so much to think about, to reason out, so much knowledge which I might gain that these quiet, all-alone hours are only blessings."

Aunt Phoebe wrote numerous such letters. Writing was important to her, and she didn't fear it. But she also knew how to live. Listen to her description of a visit to her ninety-year-old husband in a nursing home:

"I had a lot of luck this morning. I visited with Joe for one hour. It did both of us a lot of good. Help came to me from somewhere and I took us both back—years and years. We had a lot of fun. We went back to the mountains of Switzerland. . . . I tagged along and we sailed on Lake Geneva and visited cities and tramped up and down the mountain sides passing goats—herded by kind old men, or women, or young boys and girls. We went on trips through the western mountains and to Old Mexico, where Joe learned to live among, talk with, and laugh with Mexican kids. We saw bullfights. . . . It was a wonderful hour for both of us. We went along a mountain stream and he panned for gold while I fished the pools to catch us a bite to eat. The fish tasted much better than those tiny nuggets of gold would have done. We wondered why people desire that gold so much when it doesn't keep you warm, it isn't soft to sit on, and you surely can't eat it. It's surely a grand condition to hope for when we can pass through these earthly pleasures free of our troublesome mortal bodies."

Mortality is our friend. We mustn't speed-read it, skimming its pages.

I still remember, and always with alarm, a sunny afternoon when I was nineteen. I was working hard on a piece about my family. A deadline had forced me into intense, writhing thought when it occurred to me for the first time in my life that my mother, the exploited heroine of almost everything I wrote, was a person—a separate, independent, individual human being who had even once been my age! I had seen her, with love, of course, but not from any distance or detachment, as a mother who did funny things like save shoulder pads and corset stays and buy fifty-dollar fur coats and even a pile of coal beside the house now burned to ashes. (Afraid of being thought a thief, she hauled her coal home bucket by bucket after dark as she needed it to keep warm.) I had seen her, again satirically, as the mother on another occasion that became a story. The family was living in the middle of the Great Salt Lake on a railroad trestle (dispatching was a fair summer job for my father, a schoolteacher), and when Sunday morning came and we were all dressed up, my father decided at the last minute not to stop a ninety-car train so that we could take the twenty-minute ride into Ogden to church. Mother wept, and the more we children crowded around her protesting that we didn't care, the harder she cried.

All of a sudden at the old age of nineteen, I knew why. Is it possible not to think hard for that long? Is it possible that not until then did I realize why Mother cried as well as laughed over such experiences?

Yes, we must pause between baskets to draw pictures—or to draw thought and meaning. Life need not be a ribbon of worry connecting day to day.

Eileen Gibbons Kump resides in St. Joseph, Missouri, where she is a part-time English teacher at Missouri Western State College. A native of Logan, Utah, she received a bachelor of science in journalism from Utah State University and a master of arts in American literature and creative writing from Brigham Young University. She also did graduate work in creative writing at Stanford University, and is author of a book of short stories, Bread and Milk and Other Stories. She taught at BYU and USU and was manuscript editor of the Improvement Era. In the Church she has taught gospel doctrine classes and served in the Relief Society. She and her husband, Ferrell Z. Kump, have four children.

The Writer's Craft: Delight in the Ordinary

Ardeth Greene Kapp,
Vernice Pere, Marilyn Arnold

Note: The following chapter is the transcript of a panel discussion given as a legacy lecture.

ARDETH KAPP: Marilyn and Vernice and I feel honored and grateful for this opportunity. We have had a delightful time discussing and selecting and deciding what we would like to share with you. Vernice and I will each present some of our work, and then Marilyn will provide the mortar that will serve to bond it all together.

To get right to the heart of the writer's craft, may I quote from the writer Gene Fowler, who said, "Writing is easy. All you do is sit staring at a blank sheet of paper until the drops of blood form on your forehead." Don Marquis said, "Publishing a volume of verse is like dropping a rose petal down the Grand Canyon and waiting for the echo."

I believe all creative work has much in common. There is something about our divine nature that yearns for expression, and it is the substance used that provides the difference.

The delight comes for each of us through various means.

It may be in working with paint or yarn or wood or words. For the writer, it is words. Words—ordinary words—put together to give meaning that has emotion for the writer and hopefully for the reader. Using just ordinary words that I have, with some effort, carved and maneuvered into place, I would like to give an account of a return visit with my father to our prairie home. At the time of our trip back to our prairie land, my father was in the last stages of stomach cancer. He wanted to return home one more time—the last time. I would like to present for you "The School Bell":

There are times in my life, moments of exultation, when I find the world so inexpressibly beautiful, when everything holds such meaning that my soul reaches out with yearning for eager indulgence and would, if possible, consume too much too fast. But nature usually holds control over the hurried passerby and reveals in measured amounts, only after exacting the price of pausing, an experience for which there are no words.

At those times, not often, but recurring frequently enough to live in quiet anticipation, the soul seems to beat in rhythm with the pulse of the earth; and echoes return again and again like the theme of a great symphony, not void of the pain and suffering which is a part of this world but returning in a larger context where an eternal balance makes all things beautiful. After our family moved away, we went back to our prairie again and again over the years to awaken echoes, however faint, of those moments of exultation—the fragrant smell of the damp earth after a spring rain, the concert of night sounds after sundown, and the faintly audible croaking of frogs as similar sounds in the distance respond in steady rhythm.

We were all aware that this would be the last time we would return to our prairie together. In the early morning as the sun began edging its way across the big prairie sky, Dad raised up from his sickbed in the car to make an almost reverent yet fervent declaration to each of us, based on years of well-grounded experiences: "This prairie has never looked more beautiful. It's at its very best for my last inspection." Though our eyes blurred with tears, they were opened to a vision that magnified any previous insights.

On that morning of reverence, as we drove along the prairie highway that disappeared over the distant horizon, the echoes of the past came flooding back, layer upon layer, like the bands of color spreading out on either side from the yellow ribbon that divided the newly paved road on which we traveled. At the edge of the blacktop, which appeared to be freshly washed by the morning dew, was a border of exquisite wild flowers tucked in among the tall grasses that helped fill the borrow pit. The flowers spread across the fence line and blended into the next layer of color.

Across the fences the green patches of grain alternating with bright yellow fields of maize and a few cultivated clearings seemed to crowd toward the base of the gray-blue foothills in the distance. This varied band of color appeared to be never-ending until it joined the deeper purple mountains and reached upward to the blue sky resting fragilely against the peaks of the rugged Canadian Rockies. The feathery clouds caught the morning sun, casting a pinkish glow over all, as if to announce a divine blessing on this sacred experience.

After we turned off the main road past Bullhorn Cooley and drove through the river bottom toward "our stomping grounds," as Dad called it, we came upon our quiet little village in all its prairie splendor. Thoughts came crowding into my mind. *Does honeysuckle really have honey in it? Do the tips of alsike clover when pulled from their pincushionlike base really taste sweet when you put them to your lips and sip? Do the wild roses ever smell as sweet as I remembered, and does soaking their leaves in a jar of water really make rose-scented perfume?*

We stopped the car near the edge of town (which wasn't too far from the other edge of town) and began our experience in rediscovery. We came upon the mound of a root cellar covered by a tangled wild rose bush and a large clump of sweet clover that we had forgotten. We saw the two big trees on either side of the gate leading to a path now grown over by grass and weeds. Occasionally we discovered things that had always been there, but we hadn't remembered seeing them before because they were so completely commonplace; but more often we saw in our mind's eye the vividness of things that were no longer there, but which remained indelibly imprinted upon our senses.

We sauntered haltingly down the gravel road past the tall cottonwood trees on the south side of the now vacant lot where the old school had been. For us the school still remained and with that memory came a chain of reflections like dominoes tumbling one after another.

Dad took the lead. "It was the old bell," he said, and we all looked in the same direction, seeing it clearly in our mind's eye. "The school bell kept us in line," he continued. "It was the bell that kept us moving." And then, as if carried away to days long since gone, he explained: "Brother Savage, an old Englishman, was always meticulous about keeping accurate time. He never varied. There were two bells," Dad went on, "a fifteen-minute bell would ring six times, giving ample warning before the final five-minute bell sounded a simple dingdong—and you'd better be there." His weakened voice increased in intensity as he added, "It's important to listen for the bell."

My sister Sharon recalled for us the recess bell that called the students into position, side by side, boys on one side and girls on the other. Each right hand was brought to rest on the shoulder of the student in front to ensure good, straight lines symbolic of the uncompromising regulations which increased our ready response to the sound of the bell and which reminded us to be where we were supposed to be. We all agreed that, for a time at least, the old bell had played a major part in each of our lives, and though it had been silenced for years, the effects of its clear and dependable ringing, like reverberating sound waves, were still deep within each of us, prompting the same regularity and dependability.

As we mused together in silence for a time I pondered the possibility of my own inner bell being silenced, if only for a moment, just a rest break, maybe. As if reading my thoughts, Dad lay back on the soft, grassy ditch bank where we had stopped and began with a familiar phrase we had all learned to love. "I remember a story in the old fourth-grade reader," he said. I often wondered why it was always the fourth-grade reader he quoted, but nevertheless I was eager to hear another one of his stories from that source which I had come to believe had no limits.

He began to tell his story, and we all leaned forward to catch every word just as we always had. "There was an old and very large Inchcape Rock," he began. "It got its name from being located just one inch below the water's surface where it couldn't be seen, and it lay dangerously in the path of the mariners returning from sea. Many seamen had lost their ships and their lives because of the rock, especially in times of storm."

By now we were eager to learn what this had to do with the school bell, and Dad continued. "There was an abbot in the small seashore town of Aberbrothok who devised a solution to this life-threatening hazard. With great care and in the face of considerable danger, the abbot fastened a buoy with a large bell on it to the Inchcape Rock. From then on the bell rang continuously and faithfully with the motion of the waves of the sea."

Over the years Dad had developed a style of storytelling that made the pauses the greatest moments for learning. He waited for us to envision the details, then went on. "When the mariners would come within hearing distance of the bell on Inchcape Rock"—his explanation broke into a rhyme— "they would bless the Abbot of Aberbrothok.

"Ralph, the Rover, was a bit of a pirate, and he disliked the abbot and disliked even more the praises the abbot received from the mariners whose lives he'd spared. So one day Ralph, the Rover, cut the bell from the Inchcape Rock." And the rhyme continued:

> *Down sank the Bell with a gurgling sound;*
> *The bubbles rose, and burst around.*
> *Quoth Sir Ralph, "The next who comes to the Rock*
> *Won't bless the Abbot of Aberbrothok."*
>
> *Sir Ralph, the Rover, sailed away,*
> *He scoured the seas for many a day.*

More narrative followed. "On his way back it was night and the sea was high, and he thought the moon would be up. And in the darkness he said with great anxiety (but only to himself), 'I wish I could hear the bell of the Inchcape Rock.'"

> *Sir Ralph, the Rover, tore his hair;*
> *He cursed himself in his despair.*
> *The waves rush in on every side;*
> *The ship is sinking beneath the tide.* *

As always, Dad's stories stood without editorializing, left for the mind of those so choosing to explore its meaning. I thought again of the inner bell, but this time rather than wishing to silence its constant peal, I felt myself strain a little that I might hear it more clearly.

---

*Robert Southey, "The Inchcape Rock."

We interrupted our rediscovery for a time so that Dad could have a rest for his body—but his thoughts continued to feed us. At times those thoughts seemed unrelated; it was left to each of us to pick them up, string them on a common thread, and then see them in relationship, as jewels of eternal worth.

After our morning adventure, Dad stretched out on the couch in the home where we had arranged to stay for a few days. Without introduction, as if time for teaching might be running short, he quoted, "For if the trumpet give an uncertain sound, who shall prepare himself to the battle?" (1 Corinthians 14:8.)

At that moment I recalled a gift presented to me by my father months before—a small, beautifully cut crystal bell. Adding this to the scripture and the common thread of thought, I wondered if there was a message originally intended that I had only now discovered. Yes, there was, I decided; and I wondered about other lessons yet to be discovered.

On the morning that we said our farewells to dear friends, looked once more at precious surroundings, and then headed eastward down the paved highway which had replaced the dusty, old gravel road we remembered so well, I sensed the apex of this sacred happening. "I'm ready to go home now," Dad said, looking straight ahead as far as the eye could see, out to where the sky came down to meet the horizon as the sun was just rising in all its prairie splendor.

I found myself attentive, listening, wanting to share something of this moment of sweet hurting; and from deep inside, a distant sound like a divine echo could be heard ringing. A bell, I thought. Maybe the fifteen-minute bell to prepare us so that we might each be in our place when the day begins. (Ardeth Greene Kapp, *Echoes from My Prairie,* Bookcraft, 1979, pp. 93-99.)

MARILYN ARNOLD: We respond very readily to Ardeth's flowing rhythms and to places and people from our own pasts that her work calls up. Her appeals to sights, sounds, and smells put us in touch with our own surroundings and memories.

I could say many things about Ardeth's delightful narrative, but let me deal with just two aspects of her method—her use of a central symbol and her repetition of a figurative image. These kinds of things do not happen by accident; they are planned by the writer to tie the work together and give emphasis to an ideas.

The central symbol, of course, is the bell. There are actually three bells in this narrative—the school bell, the bell in the tale of Inchcape Rock, and the tiny crystal bell given to the narrator by her father. Each of these bells represents itself, a tangible object, but each of them also stands for something more, and each of them suggests the inner bell that the writer perceives inside her. Notice how Ardeth has imbued the bells with additional meanings each time she mentions them. We realize that she is doing this when her father, remembering the fifteen-minute and five-minute bells, says, "It's important to listen for the bell." Even the recess bell meant order and required certain procedures.

The bell of Inchcape Rock expands the symbolism of the school bell to encompass also the idea of safety; and it, like the school bell, is dependable—an ordering influence as it rings "continuously and faithfully." We come to understand that the writer is talking about spiritual safety as well as physical safety; one must pay heed to both outer and inner bells.

The small crystal bell serves as a reminder of the value of bells in our lives. The outer bells are provided by society through institutions like school and church and family, but we must cultivate personal sensitivity to the inner bells, to conscience, to spiritual promptings. At one point, the narrator recalls a scripture her father quoted: "For if the trumpet give an uncertain sound, who shall prepare himself to the battle?" Here, a trumpet replaces the bell, but its function is the same. Its sound must be loud and clear if we are to navigate life's dangers.

We could say more about the bell as a symbol, but let's move to the second device I mentioned earlier, the repetition of a figurative image that gives the work unity. Early in the narrative Ardeth says that as she and her family drove "along the prairie highway . . . the echoes of the past came flooding back, layer upon layer, like the bands of color spreading out on either side from the yellow ribbon" down the center of the road. Then she describes the layers moving out from the highway's center—wet black pavement, bordering wild flowers and grass, fence line, another layer of flowered color, alternating patches of green, gold, and brown fields beyond, "gray-blue foothills," "deeper purple mountains," and finally blue sky and clouds.

This image of repeating layers is picked up several times in the narrative. For example, as the writer remembers the old school, she experiences "a chain of reflections like dominoes tumbling one after another." Later, as she thinks of the school bell, she remembers that the effects of its ringing were like "reverberating sound waves" inside her. Thus, she very neatly links the bell and its layered reverberations with the layered landscape and her own echoing memories. These memories radiate from the central core inside her as the flowers and fields and hills ripple out from the yellow stripes of the highway. The image is picked up again when she speaks of stringing her thoughts "on a common thread." We see the thoughts layered like beads—or like the resounding tones of a bell, or the layers of landscape, or the reflections of memory.

Then in the final paragraph, Ardeth ties all of her symbols and images together as she contemplates the meaning of the experience she has related. She speaks of the mixed pain and joy, the "sweet hurting" of such experiences, and of hearing an echo (again picking up that central figure) deep inside that affirms that the inner bell is there, functioning. The writer then takes us back to the school bell, the symbol with which she began, and concludes with a reference to the blessed order that it suggests. The line reads almost like a prayer, "that we might each be in our place when the day begins."

Note, too, that in spite of the seriousness of the message, Ardeth's narrative is touched with humor. Remember this line: "We stopped near the edge of town (which wasn't too far from the other edge of town)." And remember, too, the reference to the wonderful fourth grade reader that held an endless supply of stories, the ostensible source of a father's vast storehouse of wisdom.

Does that give you some idea of how a writer works? And of how much fun it can be to play with language and images this way? Does it also indicate that writers of prose, like writers of poetry, are very conscious of language and technique? The essential difference between prose and poetry is one of condensation. The poet does not have the luxury of full discussion, but must make a few words say a great deal. The poet works by suggestion and indirection. Vernice Pere, for example, does not tell us very many things outright. She does not explore meanings overtly the way the prose writer can. Rather, she gives us hints and makes her images and sounds and word selection do the work.

Vernice's poetry may fool us. It may sound more like prose than poetry, because it might not quite fit our idea of what poetry is. It takes no romantic flights, nor does it search for exotic ideas and supposedly "poetic" subjects. On the contrary, as a mother of seven, Vernice has a life full to the brim with the ordinary. And it is about those ordinary things that she writes. But you will become aware that *her* ordinary is not exactly like your ordinary or my ordinary because Vernice has lived all of her life on islands in the Pacific Ocean, first in New Zealand and more recently in Hawaii.

Vernice was born and reared in New Zealand, living many of her childhood years in a Maori *pa* (village) in the care of a grandmother and step-grandfather. By comparison with many of us who are well-traveled or who have lived in a variety of places and had a variety of experiences, her life until just a couple of years ago was quite circumscribed. Yet she has made poetry out of it. She has found her subjects close by, the same place yours are—at home, in the community, in memory. What her poetry tells us is that subject matter and message alone, much less conventional rhyme, do not make a poem. In fact, Vernice's subject matter and message are usually very simple, and she rarely uses rhyme in conventional ways. What her poetry reveals, rather, is a remarkable way of seeing and a reverence for the word. She likes to play with language, with rhythms and sounds and internal rhymes. Because poetry is highly condensed and dependent on conscious technique, our understanding of it is sometimes aided by exploration into its methods and achievement.

Most of the writing I do is literary criticism—not exactly the sort of thing that would thrill you if I were to read it here. In fact, I am sure you would die of boredom if I hauled out one of my essays on some writer you had never heard of. So, what I will do now is play the literary critic with Vernice's poetry, much as I did with Ardeth's prose, talking a little bit about some of the poems she reads, hopefully adding to your appreciation and understanding of them.

The first poem is made up simply of a series of unified images, very ordinary, everyday images, seen in a new way when observed in conjunction with each other. Through these images, Vernice indirectly conveys her idea.

VERNICE PERE: This first one is a very small one called "Still Life":

> *White milk in glass bottles*
> *with red foil caps*
> *sits in beaded coolness*
> *near a blue china plate*
> *holding thick warm chunks*
> *of chocolate cake,*
> *and expectation echoes in the air*
> *to the sound of children's voices*
> *coming near.*

This poem illustrates very well my feeling that poetry should paint pictures—that it should show and not tell, and the poem is actually about the love that I felt for my children and how it was conveyed in the milk and cake. If I had written that love out overtly, it might have impressed the children, but I don't think it would have been of much interest to the reader.

MARILYN ARNOLD: An image is something we perceive with the senses, and there are many sensory appeals in this poem. The most obvious are appeals to sight, particularly to color. Note how the colors play against one another. The white milk is in a red-capped bottle next to a blue plate holding a brown piece of cake. The juxtaposition of colors is very important to the poem, but colors are not the only things juxtaposed. Textures are also. The milk is in smooth glass bottles and the bottle caps are made of foil—shiny and crinkly atop all that glassy smooth whiteness. Further still, wet, cool beads are forming on the outside of the bottles. Next to the white and red, completing the nice little patriotic ensemble, is a blue china plate, which we can imagine as smooth but not so smooth as the wet milk bottles. And against all that coolness and wetness and smoothness are those mouth-watering "thick chunks of chocolate cake," brown and rich and rough and crumbly—the very opposite of the cool, shiny composite against which the cake is placed, and yet absolutely vital to the whole picture. We can smell the cake as well as taste it. The full appreciation of the scene, however, is suggested in the poet's appeal to sound as the cake and milk are approached by the children, who will devour them with great gusto. Can you find a better definition of "expectation" than in the shrinking distance between warm chocolate cake and children whose voices we hear "coming near"?

VERNICE PERE: This next poem is called "Skateboarder," and it is written about my youngest son, Guy. I had seen Guy, I think, a thousand times on that skateboard, and then something happened, and the thousand and first time it was as if I perceived him for the very first time. I was immediately aware of a special relationship between us—between me and this, my son.

> *Lithe limbs brown as a pony's mane*
> *flash in the sunlight*
> *of the after-school day.*
> *A small breeze ruffles his precision*
> *planned turns as he deftly*
> *maneuvers the pebbles in his way.*
> *Now he's off-balance,*
> *the earth tilted precariously*
> *toward his young face,*
> *then a wriggle of hips,*
> *readjustment of scuffed blue*
> *Adidas that trail one gray lace,*
> *and I breathe again.*
> *He glides silently by*
> *the epitome of grace,*
> *nonchalance personified,*

> *a land-surfer on a concrete swell,*
> *in swim shorts, soccer socks, knee pads*
> *and bare chest.*
> *I am impressed.*
> *Can he walk so well?*

MARILYN ARNOLD: Did you notice that in the last lines Vernice rhymed "chest" and "impressed"? She sometimes adds an end rhyme for the sake of emphasis. Let me say just a few things about the poet's method here. There are some little devices you might watch for as she reads other poems. She begins the poem with one of her favorite techniques, alliteration, in the repeated initial "l" sounds in "lithe limbs." Notice how the alliteration captures the almost liquid smoothness of the boy's motion. Notice, too, how the poet works to balance words that sound alike but have opposing meanings, words like "precision" and "precariously."

Similarly, the boy works to maintain his balance on the skateboard. And when that balance is threatened, it is the earth that tilts in this poem, not the boy. Indeed, his danger upheaves his gasping mother's world. Once the danger has passed, however, she can relax and even add a quip that nips gently at him for having worried her so: "I am impressed. Can he walk so well?"

There are many, many things that could be said about this poem's language choices and repeated sound patterns, but let me just point to the kind of detail that enlivens Vernice's work. The boy is wearing "scuffed blue Adidas that trail one gray lace." Those are not just any old beat-up tennie runners. Those are specific shoes, and you can see them.

When you have as many children as Vernice does, all of them active, life is one big long holding of breath. Her next poem is about another child on wheels, this one older but still in her teens.

VERNICE PERE: "New Bicycle":

> *My daughter rides her new ten speed.*
> *(It was a need beyond all needs,*
> *this blue ten speed.)*

She rides the road unwinding
with her feet a silver thread
thin as the spokes within
those wiry wheels.
Her head bowed over
the bent metal bar
by which she steers
her way, she stoops
low, her eyes fixed
on the ribbon of road.
The skeletal frame supports
her crouched in the air,
the metal between knees
which pump like pistons
measuring breath
or the beat of her heart.
She is a part
of this blue machine,
an integral part
of the afternoon scene
balanced between the larger traffic
all of which seems
driven to do her harm.
I am alarmed
at her frailty
perched as she is,
vulnerably,
above those silver wheels;
circles of fortune,
spinning her away
out of my reach,
beyond her teenaged dreams,
and perhaps past the momentum
of even the tenth speed.

MARILYN ARNOLD: The wry parenthetical comment, "It was a need beyond all needs, this blue ten speed," is cleverly rhymed to show the parent's kindly sarcastic view of the child's desire for the bicycle. But by the end of the poem, the parent-observer has seen "beyond the need," beyond the statable desire for an object such as a bicycle, to the symbolic need of the child to move beyond her mother's protective arms into whatever life may hold for her. She is speeding not only down the road, but into the future, into life. It holds inevitable dangers and growth; and like Ardeth's father, the cyclist's mother can only advise and watch. Notice, among other things, the poet's way of showing the link between the child, the vehicle upon which she rides, and the road. That link is established through imagery. As she rides with "eyes fixed on the ribbon of road," the daughter seems to be unwinding with her feet "a silver thread" which is compared to the spinning spokes of the bicycle's "wiry wheels." The similarity of thread, wire, and ribbon unites three separate entities into one pattern.

The next group of poems calls up childhood memories. The experiences they describe are very particular to the poet, and yet they are universal. The subject of the first is one we all know, whether the setting is a Maori village or the junior high school gymnasium in Panguitch, Utah.

VERNICE PERE: It is called "The Dance":

> *Afraid some large-limbed boy*
> *would ask a waltz of me,*
> *I'm the one who hung*
> *behind the old piano*
> *while the almost-women girls,*
> *the ones with curves where I had bones,*
> *glided over the floor.*
>
> *How I'd practiced all the steps before,*
> *shuffling over worn linoleum,*
> *dishcloth draped*
> *like some boy's hand,*
> *big band mellow*
> *from the tall radio*
> *throbbing upright*
> *in the corner of my life.*

Then, when dark arrived,
we'd go, dresses starched
with expectation, unaccustomed
shoes upon our feet.
The beat, the drum,
the lifeblood's thrum
coursing in my veins,
I'd sit and wait, aglow
in my safe place.

Amid the gaiety and heat
the doorway beckoned to a night of stars
and all my years
were measured in the bars
of a halting inner rhythm
and the music's
one-two-three
syncopation.

MARILYN ARNOLD: The next two poems show the grown woman looking back on her grandmother's life and on her own young life with the grandmother. Again, the subjects are simple ones, the first posing the grandmother's skill at the washboard against the granddaughter's childishly awkward attempts. Notice how much of the language suggests the harshness of the remembered experience for the child—her hatred of the chore versus her grandmother's resigned acceptance of it. We sense in hearing the poem that the wounds "licked raw" by the wind as the child tried to hang sheets outdoors have not yet healed, and that the adult woman aches over what her grandmother endured. She also aches over the tardiness of her own realization of the toll life exacted from that grandmother.

The second poem is different in tone from the first, but both show the woman looking back with regrets because in the urgency of her child wants she failed to perceive the magnitude of her grandmother's dreams and the enormity of life's denial of them.

VERNICE PERE: This first one is called "Thursday's Child":

Those wooden washboards would wear out
under countless collars and cuffs.
We marveled when the new one came,
its ridges thick green glass
such that knuckles would never wear down—
not in years of rubbing nor mounds
of shirts and pants.
The yellow soap a brick in your hand
you passed it back and forth
up and down the cloth
laid on that board.
How easy it all seemed. Your graceful hands,
themselves ridged with veins
laced with spare suds
drawn meagerly from that harsh soap.
How many times I turned
my clumsy fingers to the chore,
chafing knuckles raw
against that board I came to hate.
Then, into the wind,
fighting wet sheets onto wire
stretched between two trees,
I raised them high
and billowing above the weeds
of a fallow field, my hands
red and sore,
licked raw by that slavering wind,
the washboard in its metal tub
reclining mild,
almost reprieve
from nature's claims
upon a woman-child.

The next one is called "That Round Half-Crown":

> *That half-crown, round*
> *in my palm, warm*
> *from my clutching it*
> *the three-mile walk*
> *to where Roy Rogers swung*
> *his silver boots*
> *into Trigger's stirrups*
> *and rode into a night*
> *of yearning.*
> *That half-crown, round*
> *and silver, purveyor*
> *of a thousand dreams,*
> *every one beyond your means*
> *to make reality.*
> *"When my ship comes in . . ."*
> *you'd say, shuffling*
> *round the cold kitchen,*
> *coaxing the fire*
> *with slim wood chips,*
> *shifting the cabbage-filled pot*
> *to hotter spots on the old stove.*
> *"When my ship comes in . . ."*
> *and your wan look hushed*
> *the wants on my tongue.*
> *That round half-crown,*
> *King George's head glinting*
> *silver in the dark night,*
> *shedding light upon my life*
> *of ordinary things.*
> *Of sailing ships,*
> *and wood stove chips,*
> *and cabbages,*
> *and kings.*

VERNICE PERE: Let me make a brief comment about the role of the critic in writing. It was obvious to me as we began preparing this presentation that Marilyn Arnold reads poems. In the poem "Thursday's Child," about the washboard, her comment on the adult woman's "tardiness of her own realization of the toll that life exacted from that grandmother" is one of those truths that a writer will very often avoid speaking out loud—especially a poet, and yet the truth is there, in every line of the poem. If a reader is perceptive and sensitive to the human condition, there will be clues, and intuitively you will know by the language, the tone, and the imagery that that line is there.

Marilyn's observations on these poems give me the feeling sometimes described by people that there's a goose walking on my grave when she tells me what I've written about. I am constantly amazed by this ability to cut to the heart of a matter in critical analysis, and I know that many times I hide things unconsciously in the poetry, and she will pull that very emotion or that very feeling out. This process of critical analysis is always valuable to me because it brings new knowledge to me as the writer and it brings to light some hidden motives in my work; you may have noted in the poem "The Round Half-Crown," that the only real clues she worked with were the repeated line "When my ship comes in . . ." and the "wan look." Everything else is very ordinary, but she discovered it.

MARILYN ARNOLD: The next two poems deal with the poet's parents and her frustrated child yearnings to be close to them. The first poem is triggered by a photograph such as any of us might find in a family album. Caught in arrested motion are the young parents the daughter scarcely knows.

VERNICE PERE: The poem is called "Taken in May, 1945," for that was what was penciled on the back of the photograph:

> *The print is sepia toned*
> *and crackled like the shell*
> *of a biddy's brown egg.*
> *The pavement is split,*
> *the buildings cobwebbed*
> *with flaws.*

People I will never meet
are caught within a prism of time.
The woman on the left
is indistinct,
her fractured hand
holding an empty basket.
The man on the right
is only a shoulder.
It is impossible to tell
whether he is coming or going.
It is bright in the silent street,
the sun is a presence, white
about my parents.
They are smiling at the camera
in a sauntering mid-stride.
My father wears an army uniform,
his snappy cap cocked to one side.
He is swinging one hand,
a sunburst in his palm,
his right arm about my mother.
She wears a slim suit,
brown on brown,
white blouse, open at her throat,
beret on the back of her hair.
She clutches him with a confident air.
Arm in arm, they walk
through the crumbling city,
down the disjointed street,
looking like a couple
ready to gamble on the world
and stake their bet on one toss.
Then, I was six,
and loved them, desperate
with the fear of loss.

MARILYN ARNOLD: Did you notice how many images of broken or damaged things are suggested or portrayed in the old photograph in addition to the backdrop of the general rupture of war? The print itself is "crackled," and the "pavement is split" beneath the "buildings cobwebbed with flaws." Cut off by the edge of the picture, a woman's hand appears "fractured." The city itself is "crumbling," and the street on which the poet's parents walk appears "disjointed." We come to understand, however, that the most serious breakage is in the heart of a youngster who wants to be loved.

The second of the "parent" poems is about the adult woman who meets, after many years of separation, her aged father. The anguish of that meeting, encasing as it does the empty cavern of the long ago child's longing, is apparent in every line. Listen especially to the language, the choice of words.

VERNICE PERE: Called "Homecoming," this poem was written for my father.

> *I saw you as the tug*
> *yet strained the ties*
> *pulling her snug against the*
> *timbered breast of that wild wharf.*
> *For the city I arrived*
> *with smoked cod and grapes*
> *in the package between us,*
> *amazed at the years age*
> *had ground in your face.*
> *We embraced,*
> *a gull cried, the cold wind*
> *cut from the sea.*
> *Later, on the terrace,*
> *salt-caked and crumbling*
> *at the cliff's torn edge,*
> *we ate, sheltered in the lee*
> *of the wind's bruised kiss.*
> *Peeling flesh from bones,*
> *you pointed to old photos,*
> *the leavings of your life.*
> *I fingered the years between us,*
> *trying to appear wise*

> *but all the while seeing you laid bare*
> *like the fish now stripped of flesh*
> *and your bleak stare*
> *across an ocean, empty,*
> *save for wind-whipped waves.*

MARILYN ARNOLD: This poem moves me so deeply and so much needs to be said about it that I hardly dare say anything. Every line, every word, is essential. Let's read the first four lines again:

> *I saw you as the tug*
> *yet strained the ties*
> *pulling her snug against the*
> *timbered breast of that wild wharf.*

The poet and her father are meeting at the harbor, but the internal rhyming of "tug" and "snug" gives an emphasis to those words that indicates a double meaning in the lines. The tug is an actual tugboat, but it also symbolizes an abstraction, a tug of the heart. The ties are indeed strained, the human ties, and the poet feels a terrible urge to be pulled snug against her father's "timbered breast." The gull that cries when they embrace gives outward expression to the poet's inner pain, and their mechanical gesture is accompanied by a cold, cutting wind. As the parent and child eat together, the very setting echoes the condition of a relationship that, like the wharf, has been left to the mercy of time. The terrace where they sit is "salt-caked and crumbling at the cliff's torn edge," though they find momentary shelter from "the wind's bruised kiss." The kiss, usually a symbol of affection, is bruised here. Love has paradoxically brought hurt. And the shocking skeletal images projected in the de-fleshed fish suggest the nakedness of her father's empty life. The poet's horror and grief at what has become of him is stressed repeatedly. The old photos he shows her are all he has left of himself, the "leavings," as she says, of his "life." At the end we realize that the title is ironic, for a homecoming is supposed to be a joyous occasion. But parent and child, with only empty years between them, have no way to fill the vast gulf. The poet can deal with her sorrow only by wearing a mask, by "trying to appear wise." All of us have had the experience of meeting someone dear after a long separation. And we know that the happiness of such a meeting can sometimes be mixed with a great deal of pain. Writing a poem is one way to deal with such an experience.

VERNICE PERE: I wanted to comment here that I think the most valuable lesson a beginning writer can learn—and especially in the Church—is honesty in the work. A homecoming, or any experience, may have been heart-wrenching, yet because of convention that tells us that such things are supposed to be happy, we will sometimes deceive ourselves into denying the pain in order to write a poem about the event in glowing terms. In the case of this particular poem, I hope, in spite of the pain and the anguish that is obviously there, that every reader who approaches it will feel the deep and abiding love that is paradoxically the cause of the pain as well as the underlying honesty of the poem.

MARILYN ARNOLD: Let's shift moods now for one last poem. This one is set in contemporary Laie, where Polynesia and modern America come together in a happy clash of customs that may jangle older sensibilities but does not seem to bother the kids much at all. In this case, the cultural melting pot is Charlie Goo's wonderfully haphazard store, where won ton chips and nacho cheese Doritos are displayed on the same shelf, and kids come to play the jukebox after seminary. The title of this poem, "Pake Cake and Prayer," illustrates the linking of two worlds, temporal and spiritual as well as mainland USA and the South Pacific.

VERNICE PERE:

> *Goo's store sits where Lanihuli*
> *meets with Naniloa,*
> *and meet they do.*
> *By seven the kids too late for seminary*
> *or the unbelieving few*

gather in gaggles that yawn
and wake slowly on the steps
of another Laie day.
Charlie Goo comes riding
his yellow bike,
his apron white,
the cap on his head such as is worn
in the fancy meat markets in town.
He trades a few pidgin phrases,
unfolds the metal gate
from across his door,
trips the alarm switch off,
and gets behind the wooden counter
which has seemed makeshift for years.
The kids file in
hungry for pake cake and soda,
crack seed, won ton chips,
and nacho cheese Doritos.
Seven-thirty lets the seminary out
and kids parade across the chapel parking lot,
all heading for the store.
The juke-box wails I love you
into the undistinguished morning,
as they converge on unmarked roads
drawn by dialogue far removed
from scripture-chase and prayer.
The early sun shafts through the breadfruit trees
and the sweet-salt ocean is carried on a breeze
yet faint but heralding the daily Trades
we have come to expect in lives
incomplete without assurances
like pake cake or prayer.

Just as this poem ends with "assurances" made up of things as everyday as Chinese cake or prayer, so, I believe, poetry can function in the ordinary. In fact, life is incomplete, empty, without the poetry of ordinary things and the reassurances that they give to the everyday.

MARILYN ARNOLD: Much as we appreciate the talents of people like Ardeth Kapp and Vernice Pere, we should not get discouraged if we don't write as well as they do. Even they had to start somewhere, sometime. How did they discover they could write? Maybe just by doing it. Me? I discovered language through reading, through loving books and stories and words. Then one day I fell into a writing class or two, and before long I was in college and writing cub-reporter copy for the *Deseret News*. And though I have since gone on to other kinds of writing, principally the dry-bones academic stuff I mentioned earlier, I have never lost that old urge to bang out a bit of florid journalistic prose. In fact, not long ago I succumbed to the urge to write about Wisconsin, where I lived for nearly seven years. I was feeling a bit homesick for the place and guilty about all the verbal abuse I had laid on its winters when I first moved there. So I sat down and wrote about it and sent it, nostalgia-laden, to the *Wisconsin State Journal*. Well, they printed it a few weeks ago and sent me a copy. Just to prove that I also enjoy playing with words and feelings and to encourage you to do likewise if you get the urge, I'll conclude by reading it to you. I called it "The Glad Surrender to Place" when I wrote it, but the editors of the *Journal* called it "A Love Letter to Wisconsin." That's okay by me. They were absolutely right. So here it is:

I am a mountain and desert person always and forever.

Wisconsin could scarcely be accused of having either mountain or desert, but lately I have had an inexplicable hankering to ramble the shores of Lake Mendota.

When I was uprooted from my mountain/desert home some years ago and pitched into the middle of a swirling, blustering Wisconsin February, I succumbed to a despair from which I was a long time recovering. Of course, Utah has its share of winter, but the relatively sheltered valleys of the Wasatch Front are balmy in comparison with the windswept fields and bluffs of the upper Midwest.

We arrived in Madison in front of a U-Haul trailer which appeared to be pushing rather than trailing our little Volkswagen. Dead tired, we had crawled and slid through four days of blizzards across Wyoming, Nebraska, and Iowa on old U.S. Highway 30, having had enough icy skirmishes with semi-trailer trucks to put, as one of my friends would say, permanent goose bumps on the VW's whitewalls.

With such an introduction, I was prepared never to like the Midwest, and determined never to forgive it for that first winter when nothing green or brown showed through the perennial snow until April. I remembered Willa Cather's account of her introduction to Nebraska many years earlier. She was just a youngster then, torn unhappily away from her beloved Virginia and scattered with friends and family and an assortment of immigrants across what seemed a terribly forbidding landscape. Looking back from the perspective of many years, she described her new home as it was then, "mostly wild pasture and as naked as the back of your hand." She remembered that she was "homesick and lonely," and that her mother was too, and that "nobody paid any attention to us." But, she said, ". . . the country and I had it out together and by the end of the first autumn, that shaggy grass country had gripped me with a passion I have never been able to shake." (Interview in the *Omaha Daily Bee*, October 29, 1921.)

What is it about some places that makes the heart vulnerable to their tug? How is it that they win us over? Willa Cather, who may have thought she hated Nebraska in the beginning, is now known as a writer who wrote lovingly of the Nebraska landscape. And I have, as I said, a growing itch to laugh with the loons on Lake Mendota.

Theirs would be the last laugh; they won me over in spite of myself. I was not an easy conquest. For at least two years my mind was a ready catalogue of Wisconsin atrocities, and I did not hesitate to reel them off for both the natives and the folks back home. There was a three-week period when the temperature never rose above zero on the Fahrenheit scale. There was the fact that we had to take the car battery inside every night if we wanted to keep the car running. There was the wind that blew almost constantly, making 25 below seem like 60. There were the storms that plastered cars and car windows thick with ice that had to be dug off inch by inch. And in summer, which did come for a short time in July and/or August, there were the temperatures and the humidity to contend with. They seemed in a mad race for the 100 mark.

But then one spring I stopped pretending that there really was a mountain lurking behind every cloud bank, or a desert canyon down the road fifty miles. I stopped squinting my eyes to turn Dutch Elms into Cottonwoods. I forgot myself and went to watch the ice break up on Lake Mendota and pile ahead of the wind in great mounds against the far shore.

One winter I began playing on the vast frozen lakes that surround Madison, making games of fox and geese when the snow was deep, taking magnificent slides when it wasn't.

One summer I began walking in every patch of woods I could find. I found myself reverently skirting the Indian mounds that dotted those woods, starting at the red brilliance of a sudden cardinal underfoot, listening to the crows overhead whose raucous caws sounded like the barks of faraway dogs.

One fall I began riding my bicycle instead of driving to campus, where I was at various times both student and employee. Each morning and evening found me rolling along the lakeshore, amid thick oak and willow as they turned gold with the mellowing of the year.

I learned a lot of things that year, things that only a place that had not been home could teach me. I learned that the unrelenting stiffness was in me, not in the climate or the landscape, for Wisconsin bent with the will of the seasons while I would not. I learned that "place" is more than geography. "Place" has also to do with feelings one willingly calls up. Every landscape—whether city, countryside, or desert—makes its appeal in its own way. It has no obligation to please. But it will wait.

Outside my window are four large sweet cherry trees which every July we unburden of their luscious load. No such crop is possible in Wisconsin, where the winters are long and the killing frosts linger late in the spring (the tart little pie cherries of Door County on Lake Michigan are miracle enough).

Behind those trees rise tall, jagged mountains, with snow still visible even in mid-July. Just two hours south, east, or west by automobile is the desert with its rugged red rock canyons and its rough old cottonwoods marking streambeds often dry by late summer.

I'm home now, many years removed from Wisconsin. But when the first sniff of lilac graces the bright May air, my mind slips back to the hours I spent in the University of Wisconsin Arboretum, where, come spring, hundreds of lilacs of every conceivable variety literally fill the eyes and nose with the richest color and aroma imaginable.

And when someone complains about the heat or the cold, I think, "Pity, these folks are not so hardy as those midwesterners, who think nothing of a twelve-hour stint of ice fishing in 20-below weather."

And when the first frost nips the pumpkin leaves in late October, I lie in bed and imagine that if I listen hard enough I'll hear the Canada geese high above the Wisconsin marshes, winging their way to warmer climes.

I lived in Wisconsin nearly seven years. Not long, but long enough. Long enough for it finally to have had its way with me. Long enough that now something inside me yearns for the white rock beaches of Door County, and the gray squirrels chasing through my yard, and the few non-migrating ducks who huddle through the winter on the only unfrozen section of pond in town, and the great oaks that stubbornly hold a few of their bronze leaves through the worst that winter can deliver. I even long for the loon that used to play hide-and-seek with me off Picnic Point on a September evening. Who ever would have thought Wisconsin could have won me over? Surely not that loon. The laugh I hear in the distance must be his.

This final item is a little prose poem I wrote a few years ago, about and for my parents. It is titled "Reflections."

Reflections

They told me about their first Christmas together,
    December, 1930.
He was out of work and out of prospects.
She knew the floor of the coal bin was showing
    through in great splintered patches.

> *But someone left a Christmas tree on their porch,*
> *pungent and green.*
> *She smiled to remember that they had had nothing*
> *to put on it, not even popcorn or cranberies.*
> *He nodded in recollection of their Christmas Eve trip*
> *to buy ornaments with their last twenty-five cents.*
> *The store had just one left, a red one with gold trim,*
> *and its price tag said twenty-five cents.*
> *Just one, for a whole tree?*
>
> *I can still see the ornament, atop all my childhood trees,*
> *Their only gift to each other,*
> *Spilling gold down the years.*

ARDETH KAPP: The "ordinary" in each of our lives when lifted up and savored with careful sensitivity through the "writer's craft" somehow refuels, restores, and rewards efforts of the creative yearnings within. Whether it be with paint or yarn, wood or words, everyone has the substance necessary to enrich an otherwise ordinary life by seeing it in an extraordinary way and bringing forth the beauty of daily living that many people only dream of.

To each of you we encourage you to release those inherent gifts of creativity. Try, try again and again, and "delight in the ordinary."

Marilyn Arnold, a professor of English at Brigham Young University, received bachelor's and master's degrees from BYU and a Ph.D. from the University of Wisconsin at Madison. At BYU she has also served as assistant to the president and director of the Center for the Study of Christian Values in Literature. She has helped prepare many lesson manuals for the Church and served on the Sunday School general board and the general Church Curriculum Committee.

Ardeth Greene Kapp has served in many general Church positions, including second counselor in the Young Women general presidency and member of the Youth Correlation, Curriculum Planning, and Instructional Development committees. She received a bachelor of science from the University of Utah and a master of science from BYU.

A management consultant, she has also taught in the College of Education and been coordinator of student leadership development at BYU. She and her husband, Heber K. Kapp, reside in Bountiful, Utah.

Vernice Pere is director of special projects at the Polynesian Cultural Center, Laie, Hawaii. She received a bachelor of arts in English from BYU-Hawaii, and has taught English and creative writing classes. Her honors include the South Pacific Festival of Arts Literary Price (1980-1984) as well as many other art and poetry awards. She and her husband, Baden, have seven children.

Stress: A Matter
of Choice

Sharon L. Staples

We are a busy people, and we live in stressful times. Stress
is defined by one dictionary as "force exerted upon a body that
tends to strain or deform its shape; mental or physical tension."

Stress has ever been with us. In Abraham we read of a
stressful situation concerning the council in heaven: "The
Lord said: Whom shall I send? And one answered like unto
the Son of Man: Here am I, send me. And another answered
and said: Here am I, send me. And the Lord said: I will send
the first." (Abraham 3:27.)

In Gethsemane, the Savior knelt down and prayed,
"Father, if thou be willing, remove this cup from me:
nevertheless not my will, but thine, be done. . . . And being in
an agony he prayed more earnestly: and his sweat was as it
were great drops of blood falling down to the ground." (Luke
22:42-44.) The Joseph Smith Translation reads, "and he
sweat as it were great drops of blood."

These verses are cross-referenced to Doctrine and Covenants 19:18-19, which reads, "Which suffering caused myself, even God, the greatest of all, to tremble because of pain, and to bleed at every pore, and to suffer both body and spirit—and would that I might not drink the bitter cup, and shrink— nevertheless, glory be to the Father, and I partook and finished my preparations unto the children of men." (Remember the above definition of stress!)

With these scriptures as a foundation, let's now turn to the scientific world. Dr. John Adams tells the following story:

"Claude Bernard, a famous nineteenth century biologist, believed that the seeds of disease are all around us and inside us all the time, that we carry with us the potential for many illnesses. However, he said, disease does not have an effect on one's body unless one's body is in a state to receive it. Dr. Bernard believed that disease was spelled 'dis-ease'—that the body has to be in a state of dis-ease before the seeds germinate. At about that same time, the famous microbiologist Louis Pasteur was attempting to destroy pathogenic microbes like those that cause diphtheria. Pasteur, when near death, reportedly said, 'Bernard was right, the microbe is nothing. The terrain or state of the body is everything.'" (John Adams, *Understanding and Managing Stress,* San Diego: University Associates, Inc., 1980.)

What are the diseases or bodily disturbances that infect us when our bodies are under prolonged stress and ready to receive them? They are heart disease, stroke, hypertension, some cancers, ulcers, behavioral disorders, lowered immunity to infection, migrain and tension headaches, colitis, arthritis, diarrhea, constipation, allergies, autoimmunities, backache, and accident-prone syndrome.

Dr. Adams claims that many of the stress-related diseases tend to have clusters of behavioral characteristics that differentiate them from others. For example, coronary-prone people typically tend to be highly competitive and driven. They fall easily into conflict with authority figures. Very active and energetic people tend to be coronary risks. Ulcer patients typically are also go-getters, but under the surface they are holding down a strong need to be nurtured. They tend to have a great deal of hostility in their systems that is blocked from expression by their need to be loved. Arthritic patients tend to be very domineering, yet they are often socially shy at the same time.

What Dr. Adams is saying is that people who tend to come down with these diseases have different physical make-ups and different personalities from the average person. When these diseases and many like them are induced or maintained by stress, they are not easily cured.

During physical stress, a powerful hormone in the hypothalamus of the brain called corticotropin-releasing factor (CRF) causes the pituitary gland in the brain to release another hormone known as the adrenal corticotrophic hormone (ACTH). This hormone stimulates the adrenal glands to secrete a third group of hormones, called corticoids or cortisol. Cortisol prepares the body for action through several physiological changes. Blood pressure rises; blood sugar level rises; aggressive feelings increase; urge to move around increases; and sensitivity to pain decreases—we can tolerate more and more pain when we are under stress.

Physiologically, the body tries to stay in balance, to maintain a homeostasis, or internal consistency. For example, if we become very warm, our body begins to perspire in order to cool itself down. If we become cold, our body develops goose bumps to keep the warmth in and to even its own temperature. Such physiological responses as blood pressure rising, aggressive feelings increasing, and so on, are normal responses to environmental stimuli. They are normal responses to stress, a balancing mechanism. It is when the body is not allowed to return to its normal state after the action hormones have been released and have done their job that stress is harmful. When we see a child dart out into the street and we find ourselves immediately darting after him, our body instantly prepares for action. After the crisis, it returns to its normal state. But what if our body does not relax? What if it does not calm down and return to a normal state after the crisis? Then we would be experiencing prolonged stress.

If a stress message is not sent to the hypothalamus and

then to the pituitary and then to the adrenal glands, no cortisol, no hormone is released, and our blood pressure does not rise to meet a crisis, nor does our level of blood sugar rise, nor do we have increased aggressive feelings, and so forth. Nor would we probably dash out into the street to protect a child. Obviously, there are many, many occasions when our body is helping us meet the challenge. Our body rises to the occasion of stress, and that is good.

Mentally, what happens to us under stress? One of the categories of illnesses I mentioned earlier was behavioral disorders. We may become irritable, nervous, short-tempered, easy to anger, uninvolved with or distracted from our homes, our family, and our friends. We may even turn away from sanity into our own distorted world of unreality and make-believe. We sometimes call this situation a nervous breakdown.

If these mental or physical conditions are fairly constant over a prolonged period of time, we are fertilizing those "seeds" of disease previously mentioned.

Two questions that might be helpful for us to ask at this point are: (1) How do we know when we are in a stressful situation? What cues do we have to let us know? (2) What is our typical way of responding to stress? How have we coped in the past?

One theory of stress is related by Dr. Lynn Johnson, a psychologist and colleague of mine. He believes that psychological stress occurs when our models of how we should be or should act do not match our reality, when we don't meet our own expectations of how we think we should be reacting or how we think we should be according to our ideal. Let's consider for a minute what our model is for our marriage, for our children, our religion or religious views or religious life, our education, our profession, our talents, or our life-style. Certainly we all have models in those areas—the ideal that we hope to achieve. How do we measure up to these models? How important is the dissimilarity between our model and our reality in these areas? For example, stress may occur when we realize that we don't have the physical capabilities or the energy to meet all the demands placed on us. It may occur when we do not have enough money to meet our financial obligations, or when a relationship with a loved one is not going the way we had hoped, or when lack of time prevents the accomplishment of important projects or talents. We may not be able to master our environment for any number of reasons. Stress can occur from any direction, and it knows no time schedule. It doesn't wait until after Christmas.

Referring to the title of my remarks—"Stress: A Matter of Choice"—I asked myself: Why would anyone ever choose stress? Why would anyone ever choose discomfort or disease? Well, I believe we do choose them for one of two reasons: (1) the alternatives are worse, or (2) we don't realize that we have already chosen between two or more alternatives. Let me share with you some examples of what I mean. Referring back to Doctrine and Covenants 19:18-19, I believe Christ had a choice, and that He endured the stress because He understood His choice and He understood the alternatives. However, I don't know if He knew this choice was ahead of Him when He said in the beginning, "Here am I, send me."

In an example from the life of the Prophet Joseph Smith, we read in Doctrine and Covenants 135:4, "When Joseph went to Carthage to deliver himself up to the pretended requirements of the law, two or three days previous to his assassination, he said: 'I am going like a lamb to the slaughter; but I am calm as a summer's morning; I have a conscience void of offense towards God and towards all men. I SHALL DIE INNOCENT, AND IT SHALL YET BE SAID OF ME—HE WAS MURDERED IN COLD BLOOD.' The same morning, after Hyrum had made ready to go—shall it be said to the slaughter? yes, for so it was. . . . " The section then goes on to tell what Joseph Smith did. I believe Joseph Smith had a choice and that he endured the one stress because he understood his choice and he understood the alternatives. However, I do not know if he knew that this choice was ahead of him when he knelt in a grove of trees on his father's farm at the age of fourteen.

Some examples close to home that many of us face as we try to respond to Church, community, family, employment, and friends are equally stress-producing. When we marry, we do not think about being faced with a possible divorce or untimely widowhood. The choices we make at this time are not between stress and nonstress; rather, they are between two or more stress-producing outcomes. How do we respond? How do we cope? Do we fertilize the seeds of disease during such times? When we begin our families, we do not know that a child may drift from the paths of righteousness or be taken from us through death. What of the young mother who must lie in bed many months of a pregnancy in order to save the life of a child and perhaps even her own life? What of the young men and young women who respond to mission calls from the Lord when a beloved parent or sibling is critically ill or near death? What of those who have joined the Church and have been expelled from their families and alienated from their friends because of this choice? All of these are stress-producing events.

I sincerely believe that we do not choose to have or choose not to have the experience of stress. It is ever with us. Another name for life is stress. Our challenge is how to make the most of it. Fortunately, there are some suggestions for coping with stress. Not all of them will work for all of us because of the uniqueness of our life situations; however, there are some basics that will get us started.

1. *Recognize that we are experiencing stress.* We should try to understand the source of our current discomfort, the source of our current feelings, and ask ourselves if they are appropriate and helpful for the situation. It helps to know what happened to get us to this point. Stress is part of our lives. We should try to discover what part we give it.

2. *Recognize that some stress is necessary and good.* Stress keeps us motivated and energized, and oftentimes it protects us. It is an attempt to keep our bodies in a state of balance. The challenge is to be able to distinguish between natural and necessary stress and unnecessary and prolonged stress.

3. *Talk to someone.* Psychologists tell us that a major reliever of stress is to talk about it to someone whom we trust. This helps us to get a better perspective of what we are experienc-

ing and to empathize with others when they are under stress. The Savior shared His concerns on many occasions with His Father and with His disciples.

4. *Develop a strong support system.* This means investing in good relationships and nurturing our friendships. It means telling our loved ones that we love and appreciate them. It means loving our neighbors as ourselves—and telling them so.

5. *Exercise at least four times a week, preferably with someone.* Whenever we move around, we expend more calories than if we are just resting. Even house cleaning and scrubbing burns more calories than just sitting, and this helps our bodies maintain their energy level.

6. *Eat wisely and regularly.* We should avoid being members of the affluent diet club, which Dr. John Adams claims means cutting down on or avoiding refined sugar, excess salt, animal fats, cholesterol, and in general anything that tastes good. An interesting note on diet and disease comes from Ernest L. Winder, president of the American Health Foundation, who says, "Current evidence relates diet to as much as 50% of all cancers in women and one-third of all cancers in men." We are what we eat.

7. *Learn to say no without feeling guilty—and then say it.*

8. *Pray and meditate daily.* Meditation promotes and teaches control. Prayer teaches and promotes wisdom along with many other qualities, as we all know.

9. *Get sufficient sleep.* A general rule of thumb is that between six and eight hours per night is sufficient for most of us. Some need more, some less. Our bodies will tell us how much we need. A woman's body knows her better than her husband or her children or her mother or her father or her neighbors.

10. *Learn to laugh at ourselves—and then laugh.*

11. *Learn to relax—and then relax.* Each of us should try to find a way to rest within a ten-minute period. It can be done— and it does work. Ten minutes is all one needs during a given stressful situation, and if we train ourselves well enough, each of us will need only two or three minutes to teach our body to relax.

12. *Take a look at our current life-style and try to enhance it or*

change it. We don't just suddenly change our life-style. We don't one day decide just to run away from home and do everything differently. What I am suggesting is a line-upon-line, precept-upon-precept approach—and it may take years and years. To start our journey to enhancement, we need only to begin, to make one small attempt at bringing our psychological body into balance—just one small attempt.

13. *Take some personal time alone just to get to know ourselves.* We know we are doing the best we can, given our life's experiences. Each woman must believe in herself, pat herself on the back.

14. *Try to put everything into perspective.* Birth is a traumatic, stressful experience. Death is a traumatic, stressful experience. Yet, remember, we chose to experience both, as well as everything in between.

That's the end of my list. I could go on for hours. If we read the scriptures daily, write in our journal daily, do our genealogy, go to the temple once a month or more, do 100 percent of our visiting teaching monthly, fulfill the stewardship of our particular Church callings, participate in family home evening, go the extra mile, grow a garden, work in the cannery, maintain a lovely home with the spirit of love, extend ourselves to our neighbors, help with community and social projects, and provide teaching moments for our children, how are we going to find time to follow one of these suggestions, let alone fourteen?

We are a busy people, and we live in stressful times. I would urge that we follow the Lord's counsel. In Mosiah 4:27, He tells us: "See that all these things are done in wisdom and order; for it is not requisite that a man [or woman] should run faster than he [she] has strength. And again, it is expedient that he [she] should be diligent, that thereby he [she] might win the prize; therefore, all things must be done in order."

And I close with John 14:27, where the Lord says to us, "Peace I leave with you, my peace I give unto you: not as the world giveth, give I unto you. Let not your heart be troubled, neither let it be afraid."

Sharon L. Staples teaches in the departments of General Education and Human Services/Behavioral Sciences at Utah Technical College in Orem, Utah. She received her bachelor of science from Brigham Young University, and master of science and doctor of philosophy from the University of Utah. Her professional background includes service as chairman of the Department of Human Services at Utah Technical College and counselor for LDS Social Services. A convert to the Church, she served a mission to Peru. She was a member of the Young Women's Mutual Improvement Association general board and the Church Correlation Committee, and most recently has taught a gospel doctrine class. Active in civic affairs, she has been chairman of the Draper (Utah) Planning and Zoning Commission and member of the Draper Board of Adjustments.

The Scriptures: A Personal Odyssey

Eleanor Knowles

The most important writings that we have in the Church, or anywhere, are in the scriptures. When the Children of Israel were led out of bondage by Moses, they were commanded to take the scriptures with them. Shortly after the Savior's death, Paul wrote to the Romans, "Whatsoever things are written aforetime [meaning the scriptures] were written for our learning, that we through patience and comfort of the scriptures might have hope." (Romans 15:4.) In Book of Mormon times, Nephi and his brothers were asked to go back to Jerusalem to pick up the brass plates from Laban. Nephi wondered how he could do this, because he knew it might involve bloodshed. The Lord told him, "It is better that one man [Laban] should perish than that a nation should dwindle and perish in unbelief." (1 Nephi 4:13.) That's how important the scriptures were to Nephi and his family.

In 1834 the Prophet Joseph Smith was told, "Print my words, the fulness of my scriptures, the revelations which I have given unto you, and which I shall, hereafter, from time to time give unto you—for the purpose of building up my church and kingdom on the earth, and to prepare my people for the time when I shall dwell with them." (D&C 104:58-59.)

And in our own day, President Spencer W. Kimball, in speaking to the Relief Society sisters, has said, "Study the scriptures. Thus you may gain strength through the understanding of eternal things. You young women need this close relationship with the mind and will of our Eternal Father. We want our sisters as well as our men to be scholars of the scriptures. We need an acquaintanceship with God's eternal truths for your own well-being, and for the purposes of teaching your children and all others who come within your influence." (*My Beloved Sisters,* Deseret Book, 1979, pp. 7-8.)

We are truly blessed today to have God's word, given through his servants the prophets, in four books of scripture—the Bible, the Book of Mormon, the Doctrine and Covenants, and the Pearl of Great Price. And we are especially blessed to have new editions of these books with excellent study aids prepared by some of the finest scriptural scholars of the Church. The greatest blessing of my life has come to me through my involvement in the preparation and printing of these new editions of scripture.

As I was growing up, we didn't read the scriptures in our home. My parents were only partially active in the Church, and while we did have a set of scriptures, they were not used or referred to very often. I had excellent Sunday School teachers, but somehow I avoided learning how to use the scriptures.

During my two years in the seminary program in high school, I again failed to learn much about the scriptures. Our teachers in those days didn't have the excellent manuals that are now available for the seminary program, and we students were masters at getting them to talk about other subjects.

As a journalism student in college, I was more interested in editing the school newspaper and other extracurricular activities than in finding my way to the institute of religion across the street from the campus. After graduation, I worked for four years at the *Deseret News,* writing hundreds of bridal stories and women's features, but my scripture study was only sporadic. This was followed by seven years in New York, where I worked on a magazine, in employee relations in an advertising agency, and on an alumni magazine. By now I was very active in the Church—but I held activity and executive positions in the MIA, and somehow I still avoided studying the scriptures.

Then one day I decided it was time to evaluate my life and to set some goals for myself. I was not getting ahead financially or professionally, and though I loved living in the big city, my life didn't seem to have much real substance. After prayer and fasting, I decided it was time to return home to Utah to establish some roots. I applied for graduate school at Brigham Young University, thinking that perhaps I could teach young people some of the things I knew about writing, editing, and advertising. BYU's Communications Department accepted me and offered me both a fellowship and a scholarship, which meant I could attend graduate classes and also teach beginning reporting classes.

The day after school started, I read in the paper of the death of the associate editor of the *Improvement Era,* Marba Josephson. That night I couldn't sleep. Something kept telling me I should contact the Church magazine editors. The next morning, before leaving for school, I wrote a brief note to the editor of the *Era* and told him of my interest in the magazine. Within two weeks the managing editor contacted and interviewed me and offered me a position as copy editor. He also agreed to let me complete my semester at BYU.

Thus, in February 1966 I went to work for the *Improvement Era.* Over the next seven and a half years I was privileged to edit and proofread every word that was printed in the magazine, including the proceedings of fifteen general conferences. This is where the scriptures started to come into my life. Everything that goes into the Church magazines must be checked thoroughly, and this means looking up and checking all quotations, including the scriptures. For one year I also had the privilege of editing three magazines—the *Ensign,* the *New Era,* and the *Friend*—during the first year of those publications, and of training copy editors for two of the magazines so I could later concentrate on the *Ensign.*

In 1973 I accepted a job at Deseret Book as the first full-time editor that company had ever had. We were then publishing about eighteen books a year (a number that has increased until we now publish over forty). That is when I started hearing rumors about new editions of the scriptures—the "scripture project," as it was called.

Nobody can really pinpoint the exact date the scripture project came into being. The first official word came in 1972, but many people had been thinking and dreaming about it for years. Since the restoration of the Church in 1830, we have been using Bibles with study aids prepared by scholars from other churches. The dream of many seminary and institute teachers was that someday we would have an edition of the Bible with footnotes and other study aids cross-referenced to the latter-day scriptures—the Book of Mormon, Doctrine and Covenants, and Pearl of Great Price. This project was approved in 1972 by President Joseph Fielding Smith, and a year later, President Harold B. Lee gave approval for the work to go ahead with full speed.

Deseret Book was asked to oversee the printing of the new edition of the Bible, using the King James text with study aids prepared by Latter-day Saint scholars. This would be followed by new editions of the other books of scripture. Cambridge University Press in England was selected as the typesetter, because of the great expertise of their employees in preparing Bibles for publication. This is when my involvement in the scripture project began. The manuscript for the Bible, including the footnotes, was sent to Cambridge in late 1976, and the editors there began the final editing and preparation for the typesetters. At this point I realized that I would have the privilege of proofreading the type as it was set, starting sometime in early 1978.

In the meantime, in the fall of 1977, Deseret Book published a book that was titled *A Topical Guide to the Scriptures of The Church of Jesus Christ of Latter-day Saints.* This was a printout of a new section of scriptural references listed by subject.

When we published this book, we included a sheet of paper asking readers for additional subjects and scriptural references as well as suggestions for making the topical guide as useful as possible.

No one had any idea how many people would take this assignment seriously, but suddenly we were flooded with responses. Who would review and evaluate them? The Church Scriptures Publication Committee, composed of Elders Thomas S. Monson, Boyd K. Packer, and Bruce R. McConkie, determined that a committee should be called to do this.

And so, in December 1977, I received a letter inviting me to serve on a committee to help evaluate not only the readers' suggestions but also the topical guide itself. The letter, signed by the three General Authorities, also said, "This will not necessitate a release from your present position, because we don't anticipate the assignment will take a great deal of time." That was an understatement of the century!

The topical guide committee met for the first time during the Christmas holidays. As I looked around the room, I wondered why I had been chosen. Seated there with me were eight of the finest scholars in the Church, brilliant men who had taught seminary and institute classes, served as mission presidents, and had a wealth of experience with the scriptures. How on earth would I fit in? At that first meeting, I was asked to take minutes and serve as secretary. That, at least, I knew I could do.

Our committee met for about eight or ten weeks, reviewing the readers' responses as well as the topical guide. We kept saying, "Here's a topical guide by subject matter—but what about a concordance?" Every Bible needs a concordance, where, if you know a specific word in a scripture, you can find the proper reference. We were told, "Well, we want one, but we don't have anyone preparing it yet." So our recommendation finally was that the topical guide be combined with a concordance as well as an index. Elder McConkie, with whom we were working, asked, "Well, who will do this work?" He looked around the room at our committee and then commented, "I think we have the talent right here in this room."

Starting in March 1978, four members of our original committee and I met every morning in Deseret Book's offices to work on the new topical guide with concordance and index. Alma Gardner, a retired seminary administrator, was chairman, assisted by Edward J. Brandt from the University of Utah Institute of Religion; George Horton, seminary administrator; and Bruce Harper, an editor in the Church Editing Department. Brother Brandt took the assignment of going through a concordance published by the American Bible Society and selecting the concordance entries. Brother Horton went through the topical guide and crossed off references that weren't as helpful and added others. Then Brother Gardner and Brother Harper merged the scriptures and added index entries and cross-references.

As the committee completed twenty or thirty pages, I would go over them, do some editing, and give them to typists. A proofreader would doublecheck the work of the typists, and I would then do the final proofreading. Eventually we had more than 1,850 pages of manuscript.

By July the committee had finished its work (we were to have the manuscript in the hands of the editor at Cambridge University Press in September), and the final typing and proofreading were being completed. Though I had looked up many scriptures as I proofread the manuscript, I had a nagging feeling that we needed to have *all* of them rechecked. To be on the safe side, we found forty people who were willing to take up to fifty pages each and look up every single scripture. We offered them a small honorarium, which most of them donated to the Jordan River Temple fund. As the pages came back to me, I did some final editing. Finally, in late September we were able to send the manuscript to England.

In the meantime we also were receiving packages of Bible proofs every week from Cambridge. They had already been read at least three times by Cambridge's proofreaders. I had two proofreaders read everything, and then I took all of the corrections and went through every page, put the corrections on the master copy, and also proofread many of the pages myself to be sure everything was as it should be. It is amazing how the Spirit works on us when we are engaged in the Lord's work. Often I'd see something and think, "That doesn't sound quite right," and I would check it and sure enough, there would be a problem—perhaps a semicolon that should have been a colon, or a letter in the wrong typeface.

By this time we were way behind schedule, and so in the fall of 1978 I had the opportunity of going to Cambridge, England, to work on the scriptures with Cambridge University Press, one of the most thrilling experiences of my life. It was not a vacation. I was accompanied by William James Mortimer, general manager of Deseret Book, and Dr. Ellis Rasmussen, dean of religious instruction at BYU. Sister Rasmussen also went with us, and we put her to work proofreading. We worked together for nearly three weeks in Cambridge's offices, and then the others returned home and left me in Cambridge for an additional two weeks. My hotel set up a table next to the window in my room, and I did much of my work right there in those tight quarters. We still were way behind schedule, and it was getting close to Christmas. Cambridge had not yet started typesetting the topical guide, so I came home for Christmas with the understanding that I would go back as soon as they were ready for me again. They sent me proofs through the next two months, and in March 1979 (only six months from our publication date), I returned to Cambridge for an additional three weeks, again working long hours in my hotel room.

Though I did get one or two trips into London to visit the theater, most days I would get up at six in the morning, proofread for an hour or so, get dressed, have breakfast in my room, work for another two or three hours, go for a walk while the maid cleaned the room, work for another hour, go out for lunch, come back and read some more—and continue until 10 o'clock at night, because we had to have these scriptures printed on schedule. In the fall of 1979, the seminaries would start a new course of study on the Old Testament, and they had to have the new editions of the Bible.

Well, we made it—only two weeks late. The Bibles were due in August and they were delivered in September.

When I came home from my trip to Cambridge in March 1979, I knew what was ahead of us. I had gone through it with the Bible. I asked, "What are we going to do about the triple combination now? Let's set some deadlines. Let's start working on it now so that we're not caught in a bind." I also kept asking, "What are we going to do about the indexes?" The old indexes in the triple combination were very inadequate. Though the Book of Mormon is the history of God's dealings with His people on the American continent, if we were to look under "God" in the old edition of the Book of Mormon, we would find only ten scriptures mentioned.

Members of the Scriptures Publication Committee asked, "Well, what do you recommend?" I replied, "I don't know of any better group to look at this than the committee that prepared the topical guide." And so in January 1980, some eighteen months from publication date for the new triple combination, the topical guide committee was called again, this time to decide what to do about the indexes in the triple combination. The committee's recommendation was that one index be prepared for the triple combination, combining the entries in the Book of Mormon, Doctrine and Covenants, and Pearl of Great Price, with the three books differentiated by paragraphing.

Again the Scriptures Publication Committee asked, "Who is going to do this work? We think that you're the ones to do it." And so once again, our topical guide committee went to work preparing the index. If we'd had enough time, computers might have helped us, but we had only three months to complete the work, and it would have taken much of that time just to write the programs. And besides, in indexing a great number of subjective decisions have to be made.

Once again I rounded up some typists and proofreaders, as well as forty or so scripture checkers. This time we had only 1,450 pages to check. And once again I proofread and edited the entire manuscript. For four years I didn't see the top of my dining room table, because almost all of this work was done in evenings and on weekends. (I kept up with editing twenty-five or more books for Deseret Book each of these years also.) Again we were behind schedule, and so in February 1981 I had the opportunity of going back to Cambridge, this time for four weeks. It rained the whole time. I stayed at a hotel on the banks of the River Cam, with a table by the window so I could look at the river. My greatest excitement that four weeks, in addition to proofreading ten or more hours a day, was watching the river rise and overflow its banks. Once I went into town and wasn't sure I was going to get back to the hotel again—the whole meadow adjoining the river was flooded, and the water overflowed on the road leading to the hotel.

At last the work was completed, and the triple combination was published right on schedule that fall.

What have I learned from all this? First of all, I have learned humility. I have learned that we must rely on the Lord, that we can't do these things by ourselves. With so many thousands of scriptures to be checked every day, I found that often I was able to open my scriptures to the exact page I was looking for—and usually my eye went to the exact word or verse on the page. Though I had to go through the scriptures many times, usually I was looking for mechanical problems, such as spelling, punctuation, and wording errors. And though it would have been wonderful to be able to concentrate on the message, there just wasn't time. But I'm grateful that through this experience, I am able to use to good advantage the topical guide and dictionary in the Bible and the index in the triple combination, as well as the footnotes. The Spirit does guide us when we are engaged in the work of the Lord; to that I can fervently testify.

I've found also that if we place ourselves in the hands of the Lord, He will direct and guide us. During the years I worked on the scriptures, I often felt overburdened, sorry for having to miss something that I wanted to do, fatigued, and even bored—proofreading can be extremely boring, especially if one does it day after day, often up to ten hours a day. But a Higher Power was guiding this work. To me, one evidence of this is the fact that in all of the King James text of the Bible, we have found only five typographical errors. This is amazing, considering the millions of characters and things that might have gone wrong. And those errors are minor, such as a period rather than a comma at the end of one verse in the writings of Paul. One can't really blame the proofreaders—who would ever expect to find a comma at the end of a paragraph?

I have learned that the Lord raises up very special people to accomplish His work. The men and women with whom I worked were all uniquely qualified for their assignments and totally devoted to seeing the work accomplished well and on time.

People sometimes ask me, "Are there miracles that you can share with us? What are some of the really miraculous things that happened?" To me, the miracle is that the work was accomplished and on time, though the masses of manuscript pages and proofs on my table seemed at times mountainous. The real miracles, though, will come in the lives of Latter-day Saints throughout the world who use the study aids to help them understand the scriptures. I use the topical guide constantly when I prepare my Relief Society lessons and study for Sunday School class. It's a marvelous instrument, a beautiful plan.

I'm grateful that during the past few years I've had the privilege of seeing the fruits of some of my efforts and my choices. The new editions of the scriptures came about, I know, because so many people who worked on them had invested the necessary faith, work, prayer, and righteous effort through the years, preparing them for this momentous effort. I have a testimony of the truths found in the scriptures, and I constantly pray that all who use these new editions will be blessed with greater knowledge and enlightenment in their study of the Lord's word to his peoples in ancient times and today.

Eleanor Knowles, editor and publishing manager of Deseret Book, received a bachelor of science in journalism from Utah State University and has taken graduate courses in communications and linguistics at Brigham Young University. She has been a writer and editor on the staffs of the Deseret News, Improvement Era, and Ensign. For several years she resided in New York City, where she worked on a business magazine, was an editor for a major advertising agency, and was alumni secretary and editor for Cornell University Medical College. In the Church, in addition to service on the Church's scriptures publication project, she has served on the Young Women's Mutual Improvement Association general board. She is currently a Relief Society teacher.

Partners in Progress: Women in Community Service

Jeri J. Winger

If I were to ask, "What is the most important thing in the world to you?" most women would probably reply, "My family." Others would answer, "My church," or "My friends," or "A good education for my children." A few might respond, "My job," and a number would answer, "My home."

If these are the most important things in the world to us, then our community must be the second most important, because it is there that all these things are made possible. It is said that a community is a reflection of the kind of people who live in that community. Are each of us willing to be judged by the community in which we live? If not, we don't have to move to live in a better community. We have the power to change it through volunteerism.

I am a genuine believer in the value and multiplying effect of volunteer service. I am convinced that there is a quality in such service that far surpasses that of any other. It is all very well for governmental agencies and institutions to devote time, money, and manpower to the service of human beings in the fields of health, education, and social welfare, but it is ultimately the volunteer, bringing a large fund of faith and humility to his or her task, who can really reach into the hearts and minds of those in need.

Voluntary service is a matter of common humane values, and it has a most important part to play. It keeps us reminded of the fact that we are all human beings with a common destiny, and that we all enjoy the wonderful freedom of choice to help and love one another. To me, that freedom is the most precious gift of the volunteer worker wherever he or she may respond to the call of voluntary service.

I firmly believe that volunteerism is part of our ethic regardless of religion, that volunteerism is part of our citizenship.

It is only human nature to want to do things that bring us satisfaction and fill our own personal needs. Psychologists tell us that the need to be of service is as great as the need for food and shelter. What better way to fill this basic need in our own lives than by reaching out into our communities to help solve community problems?

In community service there is ample room for individual expression and maximum use of each individual talent. As a community volunteer, we may learn more about ourselves as individuals. We make new acquaintances. We have opportunities to sharpen and expand our interests, and we become more interesting. I have never met an interesting woman who didn't have many interests.

In helping others, we help ourselves, because when we give, we gain and we grow. And the pay is good. We are paid in smiles and in happiness, which is the currency of love. It is what I call psychic income. Community work is love made visible. God has told us that we were placed here upon earth so that we might have joy, and there is no greater joy than that which is found in service to others. We have God's promise that what we give will be given back many times over.

Richard L. Evans, who served as president of Rotary, International, said that in order for an individual to enjoy a complete and full life, that life must include four facets: the family, a vocation (a woman's vocation may be that of home-making), church activity, and community service. So if we want to have a complete, fulfilled, and satisfying life, we must become involved in community service. It has been said that the community service we give is the rent we pay for the privileges we enjoy as citizens of this blessed nation.

From early Puritan households to modern suburbia, the strength of America has always been the family. The face of any nation mirrors the family life of her people, for the home is the child's first country and the family the first citizenry.

Where there is love at home, there will be love of country.

Where there is trust at home, there will be trustworthiness in business.

Where there is freedom to communicate honestly within the family, there will be courage to communicate honestly in politics.

To make America better, then, let us turn to ourselves. Let each individual family—which is part of the collective American family—strive for love, trust, and communication, and for the balance of body, mind, and spirit that makes for personal wholeness and national wholesomeness.

More and more we need to look to the family in the building of the individual and national character. Good families help build good communities; good communities strengthen family life; and a stable family life contributes to the development of emotionally and socially healthy and responsible adults. These are more than high-sounding platitudes—they are truisms that should be heeded.

In general, people have the same standards as their parents. Inasmuch as the center of the home is the woman, she usually sets the standards for good and determines and establishes the basic values of the family.

The home is the center of all activity. Even the president of the United States goes home, and when he does go home, it is the most important place in his life.

America will always be strong and good as long as women are strong and good. Women have been called keepers of the culture. As women and as wives and mothers, we can nurture a spirit of community service by first creating a spirit of volunteer service to one another in the home and then going outside the family into the community.

As Albert Schweitzer declared, "Example is not the *best* teacher, it is the *only* teacher." So we can best teach the responsibilities of community service by serving in the community ourselves and involving our families in that service.

The world in which our children and future generations will live demands that we be informed, active, caring citizens. If we recognize this responsibility, we will accept the challenge to do something, because responsibility implies responsiveness to need. I believe that American women will be called to account if they do not assume the responsibility of citizenship that is their right and privilege.

We hear so much about apathy these days. I heard recently that a television interviewer stopped a woman on the street to ask what she thought was the most serious problem, ignorance or apathy. Her reply was, "I don't know, and I don't care." Too often we have wrapped ourselves in the safe cocoons of our close circle of friends, our immediate families, and our television sets.

As women, we need to care enough to become deeply involved in mankind. We can't pull ourselves into shells, isolate ourselves, and let the world go on around us. A woman can't confine herself to her home and just expect that all will be right with the world. It is her responsibility to get out and *make* things go right. We cannot say, "It is not my problem," or "It's a problem for the government," because when we do, we are really saying that we've hired our Good Samaritan; we've hired a keeper for our brother. We cannot ignore our personal responsibility for attacking human and social problems. We can each of us make our own small but splendid efforts that are significant.

No one can be more effective than a woman. The fact that we are women makes us look at things in a special way. By nature, women have a tendency to be swayed by emotion. This characteristic, usually a blessing for the world, can sometimes be a handicap for us. Occasionally a woman's emotions may interfere with her being an objective citizen. We must recognize this and avoid being too emotional when important issues are at stake. We must not allow our emotions to interfere with our being objective. We must think things through clearly and carefully so that we can strike a balance between reason and emotion—be firm but not rigid.

Most women today recognize they are in better control of their destinies than women have been at any other time in history. They set higher standards for themselves, and more is expected of them. Many are setting more rigid personal goals, but they also seek to become more useful citizens in their communities and in the nation.

Each of us, as members of the Relief Society, is a leader, and each must take her place as a patriot. Our voices must be heard in the forums that are open to us—in the PTA, in church, in the schools, in civic organizations to which we belong, and especially in our families. We must make certain that our children know what our values and convictions are.

Throughout our history, Americans have always extended their hands in gestures of assistance. They helped build a neighbor's barn when it burned down, and then formed a volunteer fire department so it wouldn't burn down again. They harvested their neighbor's crop when he was injured or ill, and they raised school funds at quilting bees and church socials. They took for granted that neighbor would care for neighbor. It is only in our lifetime that politicians have promised and government has taken over the chores for which our mothers and fathers used to volunteer.

As women in the Relief Society, our record of individual compassionate service to our sisters and neighbors is commendable and should not be diminished. However, we can broaden our sphere of service to include the total community. We can each take an in-depth look at our own community, join hands with other women and organizations to determine its needs, and then form a partnership to work toward meeting those needs. Many of our women have done just that and have built a unique legacy of partnership in meeting common needs and solving common problems.

When a group of women in Tremonton, Utah, recognized the need for a senior citizens center to serve the community and the surrounding area, they were the catalysts in forming a partnership with other civic, church, and youth groups to renovate an old store on Main Street. Their efforts were so successful that they received national recognition. In fact, they were perhaps too successful: they made the building so attractive that the owners sold it. Thus the women, building on their past experience, began again—this time renovating an old school building and greatly expanding the activities offered the senior citizens.

A small group of women in Elsinore, Utah, recognized a genuine need for a community center to provide a suitable place for the town council to meet and for civic organizations to carry on their activities. They became partners with other civic clubs, the town council, citizens, and former citizens to restore the old "White Rock" schoolhouse, built in 1898 and in use as an elementary school until 1956. The building had stood vacant for twenty years when these women decided they wanted it for their community center. They adopted it as their Bicentennial project and completed it beautifully in 1976. The center was used for a few short months; then in 1977 a tragic fire burned the roof and destroyed a great deal of what had been done. This same group of dedicated women had the courage to again serve as the catalyst in working with other organizations and re-restoring the building. It now fills a need and adds beauty and dignity to that community.

A young Mormon woman played a major role in the establishment of a children's receiving home in Billings, Montana. Before the home was in operation, city officials often had to take abandoned children into their own homes. Now a new arrival at the well-kept home is always met with a cheerful smile at any time of day or night. What started as a labor of love on the part of the members of this woman's club is now a community endeavor, with each club member responsible for a specific phase of the home's operation. These women exhibit their motherly concern and personal interest in the children by giving them the fun of field and shopping trips, excursions to various community and cultural events, and dinners in their homes. To be responsible surrogate parents to the thousands of children who have been cared for at the receiving home has taken love, energy, and untiring devotion.

Unhealthful waste water and sewer conditions became so severe in Basin, Wyoming, that the women would have to put on boots to go out in their yards to hang their laundry on the line. Realizing that these conditions posed a genuine threat to the health of the community, a Latter-day Saint woman and the civic club to which she belonged marshalled the support and the resources of the entire community to install new pipelines and clean up and beautify the community. The women received national recognition for their efforts.

Several years ago, a woman's civic club in Provo, Utah, identified the need for a cultural center in the city that would serve as a meeting place not only for its own members, but also for social and cultural events for the entire community. Three Latter-day Saint women were so dedicated to the project that they and their husbands signed personal notes to raise funds for construction of the beautiful Provo Women's Cultural Center, which is now paid for and is enjoyed by many families and groups.

Founded as an emergency room by a woman's club in 1923, Doylestown Hospital in picturesque Bucks County, Pennsylvania, is now a modern 183-bed full-service facility. This not-for-profit hospital involves some 800 adults and teenagers who volunteer 65,000 hours each year, performing 28 different services under the direction of the women who own and operate the hospital. This service is given in order to provide optimum hospital services for the community at the lowest possible cost. This project has a long history of community service, and in its contemporary activities it anticipates the future needs of the community. It is a project that serves the poor as well as the rich with grace and dignity.

Participation in The Church of Jesus Christ of Latter-day Saints trains us for leadership, and it is appropriate that women accept positions of leadership in their communities where they can make a significant impact on the quality of life.

An excellent example of a community in which a woman made a dramatic difference is the little town of Cannonville, nestled in the shadow of Bryce Canyon in Southern Utah. The mayor of Cannonville is a dynamic, compassionate, gentle Latter-day Saint who was left a widow with a small daughter to rear. She moved back to Utah from Washington, D.C., where she and her husband had been living, so that her daughter could enjoy the sense of family she had known as a child. During a town meeting that she invited me to conduct, the citizens identified a number of community needs, including a community center, an adequate water system, a fire engine and fire fighting equipment, a volunteer fire department, new and improved housing, a town park with playground equipment and picnic facilities, and a clinic. Every household responded to the call for help, and the residents have achieved all of their objectives. Although Mayor Laurie Dea Holley had decided not to run for reelection, she had so endeared herself to the citizens that they petitioned her to serve again, and no one would run against her.

These are but a few examples of the significant contributions by women becoming partners in progress through community service.

President Ronald Reagan has asked for a renewal of the legacy of community service that existed in America until the costs of big government became suffocating in its attempts to care for needs that used to be taken care of by volunteers. In a television interview, he was asked what he considers the greatest threat to America. He didn't cite any foreign power or economic challenge. Rather, he said, "The greatest threat is that this independent people, who could help in a great national earthquake in another country and could bring help where there was famine—these people who have organized voluntarily to support the humanities and arts—have let government encroach more and more." He also said, "When I spoke about a new beginning, I was talking about much more than budget cuts and incentives for savings and investment. I was talking about a fundamental change in the relationship between citizen and government—a change that honors the legacy of the founding fathers and mothers, then draws upon all our strengths as leader of the free world as we approach the twenty-first century."

To accomplish this, President Reagan created a task force. It was my honor to be appointed to the forty-four-member President's Task Force on Private Sector Initiatives and to be appointed to serve as chairman of the Community Partnerships Committee. On December 2, 1981, we were invited to have lunch with the President at the White House, at which time he made the public announcement of the appointment of the Task Force. At that time he stated:

The greatness of America lies in the ingenuity of our people, the strength of our institutions, and our willingness to work together to meet the nation's needs.

What we are asking you to do is to help rediscover America—not the America bounded by the Potomac River, but the America beyond the Potomac River. The America whose initiative, ingenuity, and industry made our country the envy of the world. The America whose rich tradition of generosity began with simple acts of neighbor caring for neighbor.

We are asking you to build on this heritage to encourage still greater contributions of voluntary effort and personal involvement, and to form a strong and creative partnership between the private sector and its public servants for the economic and social progress of America.

You can help revive the sense of community which has been the hallmark of America, but which recently has been weakened by the growth of big government.

The most powerful force in the world comes not from balance sheets or weapons arsenals, but from the human spirit. It flows like a mighty river in the faith, love, and determination we share in our common ideals and aspirations.

We urge others to take part because we believe in ourselves, in those we help, and in our ability to produce positive change.

We want an American partnership that includes every community in our nation.

I feel that my chairmanship of the Community Partnerships Committee is a grave responsibility, because we know that relying on government alone to solve our problems has proved ineffective. We also know now that if these problems are to be solved, each of us must be part of the solution. And there is no better place to begin than in the communities where we live and work.

Our task force is sounding the call to build an American

partnership true to our legacy of neighbor caring for neighbor and dedicated to meeting a challenging future with all the remarkable resources at our people's command. We are working to join the strength and ingenuity of private America with the power of government in the service of the American people.

This, then, is the American partnership. Its members are individual citizens and families, civic and religious groups, businesses, unions, philanthropic organizations, trade associations, service clubs, educational institutions, and other private sector groups, as well as government leaders.

Working together in a partnership with others gives broader vision, the inspiration of united effort, and greater strength to accomplish common goals. The American spirit of neighborhood is like a communion of hearts that encircles the country. It offers a wealth of concern, talent, and energy ready to be tapped. We can go just as far as our imagination and inspiration take us.

A number of our General Authorities have encouraged us to become a part of the community decision-making process to ensure that we will have the quality of life we desire for ourselves and our families. President Spencer W. Kimball, keynoting an awards ceremony recognizing outstanding achievement in community progress throughout the state, urged everyone, both men and women, to involve their families in community service.

My family and my church are the two principal reasons I am involved in community service today. My parents set the example to us of community service and taught us that it is better to give than to receive. I want my daughter and her children to have the best possible world, and it is my responsibility to help make that world a good world.

I feel that as a woman, and having worked for so many years as a volunteer, I bring to my profession as a community development specialist on the staff of Utah State University a sensitivity to the human needs of the people in our communities throughout the state. Although there may be some initial surprise that I am in a role that is not traditionally held by a woman, I feel I am well accepted in the communities in which I work and have built up good rapport with the people because they know I am genuinely interested in them and that I care about helping them to solve their problems.

I am deeply grateful for the privilege I have had of serving as a leader in the auxiliaries of the Church. I firmly believe such experiences have provided the best possible training I could have received to prepare me and to give me the courage to assume the leadership of the largest organization of volunteer women in the world, the General Federation of Women's Clubs with ten million members in the United States and forty-six other countries. As the only Latter-day Saint to serve as an officer of this great organization, I have desired to always be an example of Mormon womanhood at its best. I have had the golden opportunity to explain the gospel to many throughout the United States and from many other countries.

I love the gospel, and I know that by living its truths, we can be a blessing and an inspiration to those with whom we associate. By adhering to the principles of the gospel, we can achieve our potential as children of God if we strive always for excellence in all that we do.

In our pursuit of excellence, we can fill our lives and the lives of others with kindness, beauty, compassion, understanding, and selfless service. We can give thanks for each new day to grow and progress and share our caring with others. We can give thanks at the end of each day for the opportunities that came to us and be grateful that we stood up to the challenge. We can also give thanks for this land of liberty in which we, as women, can play such an important part.

The world's hope is America's future. America's future is in our dreams. Let us help make them come true. If we believe in ourselves and in the God who loves and protects us, together we can build a society more humane, more compassionate, and more rewarding than any ever known in the history of mankind.

Jeri J. Winger will be installed in June 1984 as international president of the General Federation of Women's Clubs, the largest or-

ganization of volunteer women in the world, with ten million members in the United States and forty-six other countries. She has held numerous positions with local, state, and national volunteer organizations, including the President's Task Force on Private Sector Initiatives, for which she is chairman of the Community Partnerships Committee. She is also on the board of directors of the American Foundation for Volunteerism, a member of the National Traffic Safety Administration's Traffic Safety Coalition, and the national board of directors for Justice for All. For the past ten years she has been a community development specialist for Utah State University. She has held many teaching and administrative positions in the Church and has served in PTA. She and her husband, Wendell, reside in Springville, Utah. They have one daughter.

Finding Our
Peace on Earth

Elaine Cannon

Along with the lovely music of that sacred first Christmas generations ago, artists have shared the elements of the Nativity in their paintings and sculpture, and poets have written praise. One wrote what he supposed the Savior Child might have mused in the manger:

I am the Child.
All the world awaits my coming.
All the earth watches with interest
To see what I shall become.
Civilization hangs in the balance,
For what I am the world of tomorrow will be.[1]

I am interested in the suggestion of the poet that civilization hangs in the balance, and that what Christ is, the world should become.

My understanding of the Savior has been heightened

---

[1]Old English religious poem, source unknown.

through the experiences of life, through prayer and study, through yearning after His help as I serve, and through repeated precious visits to that little town of Bethlehem and the places dear to Him. We love someone more as we come to know important things about that person, don't we? I have been where Jesus lived. I've walked where He walked. I've been to Gethsemane, Golgotha, and the Garden Tomb. I know how He feels about the vital issues of life—it's in the scriptures. I know Him enough to surely testify of the beauty and truth of His mission and His goodness from birth through the Resurrection and in the continuing guidance He gives us today. I know it is through Him that our peace comes.

Let's consider some stark realities in terms of peace on earth, goodwill toward men.

> *Christopher Daniels turned into his drive*
> *With a definite feeling of dread.*
> *He hoped against hope that the routine had changed*
> *And the kids would be safely in bed.*
> *He wondered if maybe the house would be neat*
> *And his supper just once done on time.*
> *He pictured a wife, sweet and smiling, with whom*
> *He could plan his professional climb.*
> *But daydreams were gone with the first sober thought*
> *Of just how it really would be:*
> *Eight kids would be fighting and running around*
> *And his dinner designed for T.V.,*
> *His wife so disheveled and full of complaint,*
> *The problems all named one by one.*
> *His day wouldn't matter—*
> *Her only concern was to discipline daughter or son.*
> *He parked the car slowly and entered the house*
> *Like a martyr resigned to his doom.*
>
> *The first thing he noticed and couldn't believe*
> *Was the lovely, immaculate room.*
> *The house was so quiet and calm and serene,*
> *And the promise of food filled the air.*
> *He looked for confusion and clutter and noise,*

But serenity reigned everywhere.
He found his wife smiling and neat as a pin—
He didn't know quite what to say.
She smiled at his question, "Where are the kids?"
"They're gone, dear, I gave them away."
                                    —Luana Buhler Hunter

Now this is just whimsy, of course, with just enough truth in it to make us smile a bit. But the truth of it is, our human relationships are truly no laughing matter.

In one of the productive stakes of The Church of Jesus Christ of Latter-day Saints (and I give the full title to remind us of the *level* of this organization), a father and a married son have been attending the same priesthood quorum for fifteen years and haven't spoken to each other. Time is running out. Joys are missed. Surely their wives and family members are frustrated. There is no peace when families don't live in love.

These lines by Carol Lynn Pearson lend another interesting perspective to our personal struggle for peace:

Marilyn had a job—
Working out her salvation.
It wasn't nine to five.
It was nine to nine
In twenty-four-hour shifts.

And there was no vacation. . . .

She didn't have much fun
On the job.
It was more the retirement
Benefits she was there for,
The mansion, the glory.

On a typical day
She ran frantically
From the visual aid department
To the wheat-grinding
And quilting department
To the grow your own

Vegetables department
And the sew your own
Children's clothing department
And the physical fitness
Department.

She even stopped running
Past the genealogy department
and locked herself in
Until she got something done.

And then she ran
To the food storage department,
Ran with scriptures
On cassette in hand,
Ran because there were
Twenty-two minutes left to fill,
Ran past the boss's memo
On the bulletin board:

"Urgent to Marilyn:
Peace, be still."[2]

What about nations? What about peace in the world? In an address entitled "Renewing the United States Commitment to Peace," given before the United Nations recently, Ronald Reagan, president of the Promised Land, said these things, among others:

The United Nations was founded following World War II to protect future generations from the scourge of war . . . to replace a world at war with a world of civilized order . . . *where freedom from violence prevailed.* Whatever challenges the world was bound to face, the founders intended this body to stand for certain values, even if they could not be enforced, and to condemn violence, even if it could not be stopped.

This body [United Nations] was to speak with the voice of *moral authority.* That was to be its greatest power.

But the awful truth is that the use of violence for political gain has become more, not less, widespread in the last decade. Events of recent weeks have presented new, unwelcome evidence of brutal disregard for life and truth . . . on how divided and dangerous our world is, . . . how quick the recourse to violence. . . .

---

[2]Carol Lynn Pearson, "Urgent to Marilyn," *A Widening View* (Salt Lake City: Bookcraft, 1983), pp. 20-21. Used by permission.

In the movie *Gandhi*, on the life of Mohandas K. Gandhi, do you recall the dramatic and terrifying scenes of violence that erupted between the Hindu, Moslem, and other factions after India won independence from Britain? That was the violence that thrust Gandhi into his final fast before an assassin killed him. During these wicked times there was brought to Gandhi, the peacemaker, a Hindu man who tried to justify his own brutal actions on the basis that others had murdered his little son. The weakened and discouraged Gandhi gently explained to the man that the only way out of the hell the man said he was feeling was to find a little boy about "so high," and, said Gandhi, "take him into your own home to raise. Only make sure that he is a Moslem child and that you raise him as a Moslem."

A few years ago a group of us enjoyed a pre-Christmas pilgrimage to the Holy Land. One particular day was long and tiring, and night had settled in. We made a rest stop at a lonely roadside inn. It was very late and very dark as we waited aboard the bus, with the only light coming from its parking lights. No one seemed to be around until out of the night, through the dirt, a child dragged on useless legs toward our bus. He was ten or eleven years old. Some said that probably his legs had been deliberately mangled in infancy so that his inevitable beggar's life might be more lucrative.

I was conducting this particular tour bus, so I was standing by the front door as the boy approached. Covered with dust, filthy, ragged, and pitiful, he reached up in the age-old gesture for the proverbial alms. We had been warned about not giving to beggars, but the situation was demanding, and the people were warm-hearted Mormons fresh from the land of the Good Samaritan. Quickly the hat was passed for American dollars and uneaten lunches prepared by our cruise-ship kitchen and not to our picky taste. I passed these goods out of the door into the hands of one of God's little children who eagerly took them into his lap. Oh, it was Christmas, indeed!

And then suddenly out of the darkness raced other beggars who beat upon the boy and stole our gifts to him. The native bus driver was angry at *us* and closed the door—for our own good. The boy lay bleeding there until a man came out of the inn and scooped him up into his arms and quickly sped away.

This was a grim experience and a bitter lesson. Though our intentions were good, we learned that good intentions do not a heaven make. Passing out gifts is not a solution nor a substitute for the real intent of this season.

Then what of frankincense and myrrh? What of the babe born in Bethlehem? It is indeed heartbreaking when people live as if Jesus had never lived, as if He had never been wrapped in swaddling clothes nor laid in a manger that silent night, as if none had been touched by Him and His spirit of love and peace.

But perhaps we shouldn't be surprised that there is no peace on earth. Has it not been prophesied that depravity, hardness of heart, and all manner of wickedness, turmoil, and wars and rumors of wars will come to pass? The prophets in every generation have warned against sin and have foretold the calamities that would increase until the end.

In the first section of the Doctrine and Covenants, the Lord Himself told us He could not look upon sin with the least degree of allowance. (D&C 1:31.) He went on to say, "For I am no respecter of persons, and will that all men shall know that the day speedily cometh; the hour is not yet, but is nigh at hand, when peace shall be taken from the earth, and the devil shall have power over his own dominion." Then he declared: "What I the Lord have spoken, I have spoken, and I excuse not myself; and though the heavens and the earth pass away, my word shall not pass away, but shall all be fulfilled, whether by mine own voice or by the voice of my servants, it is the same." (D&C 1:35, 38.)

We live in a time when the prophecies are being fulfilled. We must realize that there will be no peace for *all* the world, no matter how often we sing the carols in the Christmas season. There will be no peace until the Prince of Peace comes again; and I suspect He can't come again until there is a covenant people sanctified and prepared to receive Him, as God's prophets have repeatedly pled with us to become. Our task is to pattern our lives after the example of the Lord and then to help others to come to know Jesus and to pattern their lives after Him too.

This is a reason for the restoration of the gospel, so that in the last days, with calamities and despicable happenings and with the name of God used as a swear word, there would be, in fact, a kingdom of truth where the righteous would be comforted and guided. The gospel of Jesus Christ teaches us how to be like Him—and we must persist in this effort.

Most of us struggle to find a single moment of tranquillity, let alone a lifetime of peace. To live in an ideal family or community, though, is not out of the realm of possibility for any of us. We can live in supreme happiness here on earth. We can know peace in our hearts. There is a precedent for it. It is a remarkable but true story. It is about people who would be great to live next door to.

The people in this community all repented of their sins, were baptized in the name of Christ, and received the Holy Ghost. They didn't just have hands placed upon their heads for the bestowal of the gift of the Holy Ghost, for, we are told, they did "*receive* the Holy Ghost." And so they were inspired in their behavior and dealt justly with one another in every way, and were all "partakers of the heavenly gift." They knew joy and did marvelous works. They had all things in common. Their life-style brought them peace, not frustration. They became increasingly attractive, delightsome, and fair. They were blessed in their marriages according to the multitude of promises the Lord had made to them. They built great cities and prospered exceedingly upon all the face of the land.

Others wanted to be like them and tried. "In all the lands round about," people followed their example. Both Nephite and Lamanite people—long-time traditional enemies, like the lamb and the lion—were soon living in peace with one another! The details of their highly successful civilization, which lasted for several generations, can be found in Fourth Nephi in the Book of Mormon.

How did they do it? They were, according to the record, "converted unto the Lord." They knew God's laws, they kept God's counsel, and it was wonderful.

The obvious thought that follows is that if we want to live in such a blissful state here on earth, we too need to become converted—not to quilting or physical fitness or food storage or genealogy, but to the Savior and His ways, and to be His servants in bringing others into the light of the gospel.

All civilization is in the balance, the poet said. What becomes of Christ in this life depends upon us. This is why I am enchanted with the lamb and the lion symbol of the peaceable kingdom. It is a visible reminder to try to be, as Mormon told the people in his day, "peaceable followers of Christ" because of our "peaceable walk with the children of men." (Moroni 7:3-4.) How does one make the peaceable walk? Remember, the quality of civilization hangs in the balance. Here are three points to help us in our efforts: we must (1) study the scriptures, (2) help others, and (3) pray. I know that this is no new magic formula. It is an old one, but it works.

Study the scriptures. We have heard this counsel many times, but to be reminded again seems necessary. Too many people simply aren't solving their problems by the word of God, nor are they lifting their lives by poring over those sacred words. Even the *effort* of searching out the words of God brings forth the Spirit of God, and with it comes peace. We need to pray before we begin our study so that our minds may be clear, and so that through the Spirit we may have understanding. We might read the scriptures in a foreign language, if we can; this is startlingly enriching. So is reading them out loud to ourselves or with others. We should read them, quote them, *live* them.

Our youngest daughter's husband is a bishop in a stake away from Utah, and she has been the spiritual living leader in Relief Society. They are the only members of the Church on their cul-de-sac. She was invited to join a neighborhood ecumenical Bible class, and she wondered at first whether she should participate even if she could squeeze in the time. But in the spirit of wholesome neighborliness, she has met with these fine women for over a year now. A minister's wife, who didn't want a Mormon in the group, had to be won over by our daughter's family. There were visits, tot-tending, meals taken in times of need, and a persistent warm greeting in spite of cold response. But peace has come. Prayers and good deeds and making time to meet people on their turf has welded the people on that street together. And they have confidence about the kinds of homes their children are playing in.

We entertained the executive board of the National Council of Women in Salt Lake City for seminar and training meetings. At the banquet one of the most distinguished women asked me if she could take home with her the copy of the Book of Mormon that she had found in her hotel room. We talked casually about it over dinner, and then I felt impressed to say to her what I tell anyone who isn't hooked on scripture reading yet—I told her to begin reading at chapter 11 of Third Nephi. I wrote this information on the back of her placecard and explained that since she had been taught to believe in Jesus as a schoolgirl, she would find it most interesting to learn about the Savior's ministry here on this continent. The next morning she reported to me that she'd read it all and said, shyly, "It made me shiver to read about this." Recently I spoke with her on the phone, and she said that she had sent her only daughter, who is seriously ill, to the LDS Visitor's Center in New York, which I had told her about. And then she added, "Guess what? She came home with a pamphlet that told all about Jesus coming here to this continent. Can you believe it? They knew about this in New York!"

This lovely cultured woman, who was born and reared in Europe as a Catholic with all the comfortable adornments of a sophisticated life, was excited. She had chills up her spine and a spirit in her heart as she read about the people in the land Bountiful touching the pierced side of the Savior and repenting, being baptized by immersion, being changed. She felt peace and healing because of this experience. She said that being in Salt Lake City was the most important contribution to her life.

Yes, we need to study the scriptures, and to feel the peace and the healing.

Help others. This second suggestion is based upon the familiar principle that when one is converted, one strengthens others and is dedicated to the simple, lifting, and rare idea that we all are somehow responsible for each other.

There are many ways of helping. I am not thinking so much now of service projects or gift giving as of the lift and encouragement we all need. Here are some lines that should leave each of us feeling very tender indeed!

> *Blessed are they who understand*
> *My faltering step and palsied hand.*
> *Blessed are they who know that my ears today*
> *Must strain to catch the things they say.*
> *Blessed are they who seem to know*
> *That my eyes are dim and my wits are slow.*
> *Blessed are they who looked away*
> *When something spilled at the table today.*
> *Blessed are they with a cheery smile*
> *Who stop to chat for a little while.*
> *Blessed are they who never say,*
> *"You've told that story twice today."*
> *Blessed are they who make it known*
> *That I'm loved, respected, and not alone.*
> *Blessed are they who know I'm at a loss*
> *To find the strength to carry the Cross.*
> *Blessed are they who ease the days*
> *Of my journey Home in loving ways.*[3]

Recently a new member of the general board was set apart by a special servant of God. It was a fine experience to hear what the Lord wanted her to hear about her new assignment. Afterward her family spoke of her unfailing thoughtfulness, her incredible caring, the good feeling about her. Then one daughter added, "Even the ducks answer her call." And another said, "She clears the lake with her call."

I thought about that for a moment. "Even the ducks answer her call." It's true, she is a city girl with a remarkable way

---

[3]Esther Mary Walker, "Beatitudes for Friends of the Aged."

with animals. I strongly suspect and have long predicted that she'll have some part in the settling of the animals in the peaceable kingdom. But until then, she has an impressive private record that runs alongside the public one of church and community service, which indicates that this woman understands the works of righteousness and implements them quietly in the lives of others. It is the power of God working through her to meet the needs of those in his kingdom—even ducks.

Pray. In our pursuit of peace in a world of turmoil, prayer is vital. This in itself is a lengthy subject, but it is a great blessing to us when we arrange our lives so that we have ample quiet time alone with God. We must give God quality time when we are both awake and alert.

Recently I visited the home of an unmarried young woman whose career keeps her deeply involved with federal government affairs. Her home is a basement apartment. The decor is eclectic, with handsome art and early attic furniture. There is a wonderful spirit there; I felt it moments after I went in. She lives alone, but it is a home. Bread was baking—she's always baking bread for someone downtown. Piled high upon the desk were albums of photos and cases of slides, pictures of her widely extended family. The scriptures beside her bed were well used, underlined. Other Church literature was nearby. But it was the spirit there that touched me most. I felt peace, as if angels attended her. We talked about that together. Her home had been dedicated by her father in family prayer. Her own prayers, both formal and informal, were frequent. Her closeness to Heavenly Father made her small apartment a corner of heaven on earth. She echoed the sentiment, "I believe in the separation of church and state but not in the separation of God and nation." And I might add that she doesn't believe in the separation of God and the single girl.

Some time ago Dwan Young, general president of the Primary, and I were touring the Philippines on a Church assignment in the company of Elder and Sister Robert L. Simpson. We were taken to the home of a large family of girls, all but one of Young Women age. They were living with only their mother, because the father had passed away. Home was a room made from packing boxes and palm fronds. It was about eight feet square, and the only pieces of furniture were a homemade wooden bench and a small cabinet. The top of the cabinet was piled high with old manuals of the Church that a former missionary had shared, the scriptures, a hymnbook, and the Young Women songbook. The cabinet shelves held their few supplies. The room was decorated with pictures cut from Church magazines and pinned on the wall. The cooking, the laundry, sleeping, and the personal needs departments were out under the palm trees and in the tropic brush. Get the picture now: one room with the simplest of furnishings, a terrible diet I won't describe, but a gospel-centered life-style. There were seven teenage girls of great personal beauty, and a lively mother who was in some serious trouble beyond her control. When six visitors crowded in, there was no room for us to do anything but stand. It was wall-to-wall people. We talked for a moment and then the mission president, Brother Sperry, asked the girls to sing.

Filipinos love music and they are good at it. These girls were no exception. The old guitar, given to them by a departing elder, was taken from behind the bench, where they then huddled together to begin their serenade. While the fifteen-year-old strummed, they belted out hymns and Young Women and Primary music. After a half-hour concert, they announced that they were going to sing their favorite, "Families Can Be Together Forever." It was then that the Spirit swelled within us. You see, their mother's trouble and father's death threatened their family unit. Yet their faith had taught them they'd be together forever in peace, and they wept openly as they sang about it.

Elder Simpson left a blessing upon that home. The power of prayer is marvelous; tears spilled down our cheeks and comfort came into all of our hearts as he prayed. The power of God working through a special servant of the Lord brought hope into that home, and it became a place of peace. The witness came to us all at the same time that God does live and is mindful of the details and needs in our lives. He does care.

That was a remarkable experience of assurance. And we found out later that the visit was an answer to their prayers.

Prayer takes us back to Bethlehem and heralds the peaceable kingdom. Quarreling couples can pray their way into love again. Frightened children are comforted. The sick are healed. Families can have hope. The young find strength to resist temptation. The distraught can endure. All of us can employ the hard doctrine of true forgiveness as well as learn to love appropriately. Civilization hangs in the balance.

In Romans 8:6 we read: "To be spiritually minded is life and peace." And from Isaiah 32:17 we learn that "the work of righteousness shall be peace; and the effect of righteousness quietness and assurance for ever."

Let us go back in our hearts to Bethlehem—to the silent and holy night; to Mary, who obeyed the will of God in bearing the baby Jesus; to Joseph, who stood by and helped; to Jesus, the infant who grew to teach the saving principles, to work miracles, to smooth rough waters with the command "Peace, be still!" and to be our Redeemer. In the name of Jesus Christ, let us be peacemakers and help others find their way into the peaceable kingdom. All civilization depends upon it. "Blessed are the peacemakers: for they shall be called the children of God." (Matthew 5:9.) I can't think of a better thing to be called at the season of our elder Brother's birth, can you?

Elaine Cannon was called in July 1978 to serve as general president of the Young Women of the Church. A graduate of the University of Utah, she has been an editor and writer for Church publications, the Deseret News, *and television, as well as a freelance writer for national publications. She has also taught continuing education courses for Brigham Young University, the University of Utah, and Utah State University. In the Church she has served on the general board of the Young Women's Mutual Improvement Association, on the Youth Correlation Committee, in the LDS Student Association, and on Church writing committees. She has recently been serving as a vice-president of the National Council of Women. She and her husband, D. James Cannon, have six children.*

Index